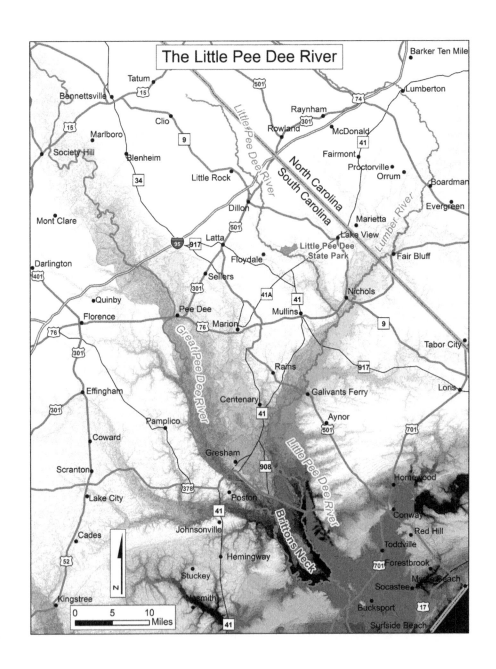

Down The Little Pee Dee

Paddling
South Carolina's
Legendary Blackwater River

William S. Walker

© 2014 William S. Walker
All Rights Reserved including photographs

No part of this publication may be reproduced, stored in a retrieval system, or transmitted, in any form or by any means, electronic, mechanical, photocopying, recording, or otherwise, without the written permission of the author. All photographs by the author unless otherwise indicated.

First published by Dog Ear Publishing
4010 W. 86th Street, Ste H
Indianapolis, IN 46268
www.dogearpublishing.net

ISBN: 978-1-4575-2917-7

This book is printed on acid-free paper.

Printed in the United States of America

Acknowledgments

I am deeply indebted to my cousin and friend L.L. Gaddy for his assistance in the research and writing of this book. He was my paddling companion for every mile down the Little Pee Dee and his encyclopedic knowledge and the generous manner in which he shared it with me were second only to his unfailing dedication to a project that stretched over two years. This book would not have been possible without his many contributions.

Former Francis Marion Trail Commission Director Bob Barrett of Florence and Revolutionary War expert Tres Hyman of Cartersville read the manuscript and offered sound advice on improving the historical material. My college friend Charles Bethea of Marion, a board member of the Pee Dee Land Trust, also read the manuscript and offered helpful suggestions. Early on, Little Pee Dee River guide Bob Jolly, Jr., of Marion, provided a good overview of the lower river. Author Norm Zeigler of Sanibel Island, Fla., a colleague from our days together at The Stars and Stripes, was also a reader and offered additional, valuable suggestions and encouragement. Norm's comfortable writing style was always in my mind as I tried to describe my days on the river.

My friend Lafon Legette and his wife Cindy, who is also my cousin, were great listeners to my stories about the river and provided encouragement throughout the research and writing. It was Lafon's gift to me of *Home By The River*, a book by Archibald Rutledge, that first gave me thoughts of writing about a theme close to home. Cindy's son, John Lane, who has found many Revolutionary War and Colonial-era artifacts over the past two decades of metal detecting, was an excellent source of information on Francis Marion's encampments along the Little Pee Dee and the Great Pee Dee.

My late cousins Ben Brown and Gene Connelly were always in my thoughts in the writing of this book. Ben's mother and my aunt, Annell Walker Brown, is a family treasure and an invaluable information source about our early life in Nichols. Ben's sisters Patty and Sandra, and Sandra's husband Joe Turbeville, were always good listeners and provided information on life in Nichols and Mullins. Ben's widow, Sue Page Brown, remains the closest of friends. Ben and Sue's children, their daughter Page and son Benjamin, know how much the Lumber and Little Pee Dee meant to their father. Page, her husband Mitch Abernethy, and their sons William, Brown and Mitchell floated the river with me twice in recent years and our experiences helped in the research for this book.

My friend and longtime tailwheel flight instructor John Whittington of Rowland, N.C., pounded on my head enough about using the rudder and other aviation essentials to enable safe flights above the river with one hand on a camera and the other on the control wheel. Thanks also to the Daughters of the American Revolution Blue Savannah-Swamp Fox Chapter for their interest in the research.

Computer expert and good friend Ruben Thompson kept all the hardware going and the software functioning during the long writing process. Dr. Joshua A. McDuffie patiently worked through more than 20 versions of the maps presented in the book before completing all our design changes and additions. And we successfully hauled our gear time after time in my old truck superbly maintained by mechanic Sammy Watts, whose farm borders the Little Pee Dee. And aircraft mechanic Ken Hanke of Clio kept my old Cessna in top flying condition for the many trips above the river.

Betty and C.P. Mincey, my aunt and uncle who appear in the book, have been lifelong supporters of my writing efforts. The same is true of my aunt, Sally Gaddy, Chick's mother.

Finally, my best friend, my wife Elizabeth, deserves the greatest thanks of all for her unconditional support and wise counsel in the half century we have known and loved each other.

To five good men
Ben M. Brown, Jr.
C.E. Connelly, Jr.
L.L. Gaddy, Sr.
C.P. Mincey
William S. Walker, Sr.

Contents

Acknowledgments v
Introduction 1
A Wet And Wild Beginning 5
Portages And Log Jumps 17
Beware Of Tame Ducks 22
A Cross For Michelle Brown..28
Chief James Caulder And The Pee Dee Indian Tribe........................35
What Noise? 41
Riding The Flood To Dillon County Landing....................................45
Nije Važno And A Rumble On The River..53
Fallen Trees Everywhere..60
Return To Mosquito Beach..66
Down The Wide Water On Quincey's River 82
Knife Island, Ex In-laws And A *Nerodia sipedon*..............................95
Pity The Foreigners At Hughes Landing 103
Into The Heart Of Francis Marion Country 111
To The Great Pee Dee Junction...121
Keeping A Promise On The Lumber River......................................133
Flying The River 147
Map annex 150
Bibliography 152
Notes..154

Introduction

Paddling the Little Pee Dee River in eastern South Carolina ranks as one of the most memorable water adventures in the South. And one not often completed in its entirety because of the difficult nature of the upper river. This Southern blackwater river rises from an old millpond along the North Carolina line and flows 109 miles through a sparsely inhabited belt of often pristine Carolina lowland forest to its junction with the Great Pee Dee River near the Atlantic Coast.

This book records a journey down the river with my cousin Chick Gaddy. I am William S. Walker, a writer with a house alongside the river at Fork Retch, S.C. Chick is L.L. Gaddy, a naturalist and author who is an expert on the Southern outdoors. I grew up in Nichols, only a scant two miles from the river and close beside the Lumber River, a tributary of the Little Pee Dee. My boyhood was spent on both rivers. Chick explored the same places as a boy and young man.

The Little Pee Dee drains a verdant belt that winds through four South Carolina counties – Marlboro, Dillon, Marion and Horry – on the way to the Great Pee Dee. The river floodplain is home to a stunning variety of wildlife including deer, alligator, feral hogs, turkeys, beaver, muskrat and at least 50 species of birds, a like number of fish plus snakes of all kinds, most notably the cottonmouth moccasin.

Tannins generated from decaying vegetation stain the river to its unique blackwater coloration. And when the flow crosses the frequent stretches of brilliant white sand, it produces images of a gold-tinted bottom stretching uninterrupted for miles.

The Little Pee Dee earned an enduring place in American history during the Revolutionary War when Francis Marion, the legendary Swamp Fox, made the region his private reserve for tormenting the British. In 1780, when the war hung in the balance with British troops on the verge of subduing the Southern colonies, Marion was the American commander who would not quit. The Swamp Fox and his small band of guerrillas struck with a series of raids that prevented the British from consolidating critical lines of communication and supply. His attacks came at a critical time when the entire American Revolution was in danger of being lost. And the first phase of his campaign was fought from the Pee Dee swamps and rivers. Under way on the Little Pee Dee we were never far from the places that made Marion and his men the state's greatest folk heroes.

We broke our journey into day trips, 18 in all totaling 160-plus hours on the river. Much of our time was spent paddling in the shadows of overhanging swamp forest, crossing under great, gray streamers of Spanish moss, moving along a waterway capable of conveying a traveler, literally and figuratively, back across the centuries to a time when the river was the domain of the native Indians who inhabited eastern South Carolina.

Today, despite the inroads of civilization, a Little Pee Dee traveler encounters mile after uninterrupted mile of towering forest, primarily cypress, tupelo, water and laurel oak and the occasional stand of loblolly pine. Knobby cypress knees, the above water roots of the beautiful and massive cypress forest, protrude from the swamp floor and line the river banks by the tens of thousands. For half its length, until it reaches the junction with the Lumber River between Nichols and Mullins, the Little Pee Dee is unsuited for all but the smallest of boats, primarily single seat fishing rigs. Thus, the natural beauty of the river is only occasionally interrupted by humans. A few dozen houses and cabins have been built along the sections closest to public roads. There are clusters of larger homes around Dillon, at Fork Retch below the junction with the Lumber and at Cartwheel Landing, Knife Island, Davis Landing and Locust Tree Landing in Lower Marion County. But the river for the most part remains as natural and wild as it was in Francis Marion's time.

Ours was not only a river journey of natural, geographic and historical discovery but also one involving the people we met on the way downstream—anglers, pleasure boaters, tourists and local residents. In addition, we involved our family and friends in the project. Our main man in making many parts of the trip happen was our uncle, mentor and frequent truck chauffeur, C.P. Mincey. His farm backs up to the Little Pee Dee between Nichols and Mullins. C.P., a retired barber from Nichols, is an accomplished farmer and conservationist. C.P.'s wife of 65-plus years, our mothers' sister Betty, often fed us after the trips along with my wife Elizabeth, a local girl raised only a short distance from the banks of the river. Aunt Betty, Chick's mother Sally, and my mother Clarice were South Carolina farm girls, Blantons from Wannamaker near Duford in Horry County.

The Little Pee Dee journey was important to me as a tribute to a brave man who didn't live long enough to join us. A year before Chick and I set out, I promised my closest boyhood companion, my first cousin Ben Brown, that he and I would get back on the rivers of our youth when he recovered from cancer surgery. But his condition worsened in early 2011 and two days before his death I vowed to him I would make the river trip for both of us. That promise to Ben was my main inspiration in writing this book.

Our journey passed through the land of the *Vehidi*, or Pee Dee Indians, original settlers of the region that encompasses this river belt descending through Marlboro and Dillon Counties and along the border between Marion and Horry Counties, all of it between the two rivers, the Little Pee Dee and the Great Pee

Dee. The chief of the Pee Dee Tribe, James Caulder, shared with me his people's cultural history and attachment to the river from the earliest times.

I kept a written diary of the individual trips while Chick, drawing on his immense knowledge of the South Carolina outdoors, observed the flora, fauna and wildlife of the Little Pee Dee River Basin and filled me in on anything he found interesting. We traveled in lightweight plastic kayaks. Chick carried a waterproof point and shoot digital. I used a larger digital single lens reflex with a zoom lens. During our days on the river we took more than 10,000 photographs and a collection of them is presented in this book.

Chick, a.k.a. Dr. L.L. Gaddy, Jr., probably knows more about the plants and wildlife of South Carolina and the Southeast than anyone you will ever meet. And he loves to talk about those subjects and almost anything else. One of his books, and my favorite, is *The Natural History Of Congaree Swamp*, an outstanding nature guide on Congaree National Park in central South Carolina written with John E. Cely.

Our youth was primarily spent outdoors in the absence of electronic games, television and computers. Chick grew up in Timmonsville, a Florence County town a bit larger than my home, Nichols, in Marion County, but still a place where everyone knew everyone else. He often traveled to Nichols with his father, an ardent Little Pee Dee fisherman who ran the National Guard Armory in their town. As a boy he was Little Chick, his father Big Chick. To our family he remains Little Chick, even as his weight flirts with 250 pounds.

I spent much of my early years barefoot tramping the forests and swamps around Nichols where my dad ran a corner grocery. He was Will. I was Billy. I fell in love with one girl in high school, Elizabeth, married her after university, and that happy chapter in my life has continued for nearly 50 years. We live part of the year on the water at Fork Retch, one of the most beautiful stretches of the river.

Despite our limited exposure to the rest of the world in our youth, Chick and I came to be explorers of sorts, visiting and working in more than 100 countries between us. He was divorced and in his forties when he first went to China to study several species of wild ginger. Less than a year later he married Hu Ye, a Chinese woman who had assisted his research there. They had a son, Lin, who is today a college student and a soft-spoken all-around good kid and young man. This marriage eventually ended but good-natured Chick and his Ex remain great friends and he also gets along well with her second husband, Tan. When Chick was his son Lin's age he took a break from college, traveled the U.S. and worked for a while at minimum-wage jobs before eventually going back to the University of South Carolina and then to the University of Georgia where he did his Ph.D. dissertation on ant-plant ecology. His specialties are plants and invertebrates, but he is interested in almost everything else that moves. He has spent the last 30 years doing environmental-related studies from Maine to Idaho and heads his own consulting firm, *terra incognita*, which does endangered species, wetlands, and conservation work. His long years of experience roaming the backwoods and swamps were ideal preparation for our trip.

While Chick spent those 30-plus years mostly in the U.S., I was overseas, working as a reporter and editor for *Stars and Stripes*, a great newspaper serving the U.S. military around the globe. I finished my newspaper work in 2002 and decided to continue my education begun at Clemson University and the University of South Carolina with a Ph.D. at Heidelberg University. The university graduated its first class more than 300 years before the United States was founded, and has a deserved reputation as one of the world's great places to study. I majored in East European history and Slavic languages, both interests developed while covering the Balkan region and the conflicts in Bosnia and Kosovo in the 1990s. My dissertation was published in 2010 as *German and Bosnian Voices in a Time of Crisis*, a book about Bosnian refugees in Germany during the war years and afterwards.

Camping out was not a part of our Little Pee Dee trip plans. Chick and I have had our share of overnights along the Low Country rivers in South Carolina, doing battle with mosquitos, wasps, red bugs, extreme heat, energy-sapping humidity, venomous snakes and most of the other unpleasant distractions present in this beautiful but often inhospitable place. We set up our trips to be the kind of outings that other boaters, especially those new to the river, might duplicate using our experiences for assistance. Despite our plans for day trips only, the watertight compartment on each kayak always held enough food, extra clothing, survival gear and first aid supplies to handle camping on the river. Although some of the day trips lasted up to 12 hours, we never had to overnight, principally because we took remaining distance estimates throughout each day and if necessary cut the scheduled section short.

We planned the journey around our regular work schedules and in the beginning estimated it would take a year to paddle the entire river. That stretched to more than two years as we juggled other work assignments. We did not hurry, exploring countless sloughs, lakes and old channels and oxbows off the main river. For good measure we also paddled a 20-mile section of the Lumber River from Fair Bluff, N.C., to its junction with the Little Pee Dee. This was a favorite stretch of water for my cousin Ben and another cousin, Gene Connelly. I also followed the river from the headwaters to the junction with the Great Pee Dee in my airplane. Eventually I made more than a dozen flying trips over various sections of the river.

On our Little Pee Dee journey the people we met provided unique perspectives on the waterway. Not surprisingly, we learned far more under way about the river than we knew at the start of our journey. From our initial launch at the headwaters, into a stream only a few feet across, all the way to the 600-foot-wide channel of the river where it enters the Great Pee Dee, we paddled and talked and photographed our way, floating mile after mile after mile through some of the South's finest natural scenery. Now I invite you to turn the page and share our journey down South Carolina's legendary blackwater river, the Little Pee Dee.

William S. Walker
Fork Retch, S.C. May 2014

The headwaters of the Little Pee Dee River flow out of Red Bluff Lake outside the town of Clio in Marlboro County, S.C. Photo taken after snowfall in January 2014.

1

A Wet And Wild Beginning

Red Bluff Lake to County Line Road (4.5 Miles)

Overnight dew still glistened on the cypress trees which dotted the dark, mirrored surface of the water as we pulled our kayaks down from my old pickup. It was February and still a cool 52 degrees at 10 A.M. My paddling partner Chick Gaddy and I were at Red Bluff Lake, an old Southern mill pond about three miles outside the town of Clio in the hinterlands of Marlboro County, S.C. There, at the end of American Legion Road off S.C. highway 83, the lake spills into a basin that forms the headwaters of South Carolina's legendary Little Pee Dee River.[1]

A sign on the dilapidated, two-story wooden building atop the dam advertised all-day fishing for $5. But there was no one in sight to collect the money.

Another paint-chipped sign warned: "No Profanity, No drugs or Alcohol. If you do not obide by rules you will be asked to leave." We planned to 'obide.'

The building on the dam once housed a hydroelectric generator, we had been told by Chief James Caulder of the Pee Dee tribe. It supplied electricity to the town of Clio for many years, he said. The spillway outlet fifteen feet below the old generator house released a steady flow from the millpond into the swirling pool below the dam. This pool of water, perhaps 100 feet square, was our starting point. Beyond it was the 109-mile journey we had waited a good part of our lives to undertake.

A single fisherman witnessed the start of our trip. He was a middle-aged, angular-faced fellow clad in jeans and a long sleeve shirt. He stood on the dam directly above the spillway and intently watched the tip of a fishing rod with its line strung out to the water below.

"Not catching much of anything," he said when asked. We had no way of knowing then, but it was the near standard answer along the entirety of the river. The Little Pee Dee has a deserved reputation as a place where anglers seldom reveal how the fishing is going for fear of giving away the location of a good spot.

We slid the kayaks down the side of the earthen dam to the pool of water beyond the sluiceway. The sun was already high in the late winter sky when we pushed off from the shallows. Our goal was the S.C. Highway 57 Bridge inside Dillon County, about five miles straight-line but probably ten miles on the river. We had left Chick's car there earlier that morning after he drove down from his home in Columbia, the state capital.

The river was at flood stage, but we launched with boundless optimism and without apprehension. We were finally under way on our dream trip, one whetted by conversations with many people who had told us they knew the river well. All of them offered advice on various sections. But no one had talked about the opening stretch. In the coming hours we found out why. It turned out few people had ever departed by boat from Red Bluff and fewer still had paddled it at flood stage. Chief Caulder told us later he had walked the banks there often. "But I never did that section in a boat," he said. "It's pretty wild."

There was method in attempting the first section at flood level. We reasoned, or perhaps just rationalized, that in high water there would be more cut-throughs, more places to get around fallen trees if the water were flowing not only in the river but also through the swamps. During the next eight hours we found out we were right and wrong on that score. In the high water we could divert into the swamp at any time, but we found there a maze of cypress knees sprouting between massive tree trunks, barring easy passage. We floated when we could, ran the gauntlet of cypress knees when we had to, and dismounted to slog across the mud floor of the swamp when nothing else worked.

We launched at 10:45 into a 25-foot wide stream already moving briskly. The sun faded almost immediately, shielded from the water by a forest canopy that remained thick even in winter. On the first bend, the river looked as if it were ending. It was, however, an illusion repeated often during the day. The channel changed direction radically, veering 180 degrees in a turn that took it back toward Red Bluff. Successive turns came quickly and were startlingly sharp, setting a pattern for the next four hours as we struggled to find a channel through what turned out to be an endless series of strainers, the downed tree trunks and partially fallen trees still growing from the bank at near impossible angles.

It was immediately obvious there would be little rest on this section, no straightforward passage down the river. We would be required to paddle hard, turn often and portage frequently. Less than 15 minutes downriver we diverted into the swamp to get around a fallen oak. A quarter of an hour later we could find no swamp channel at another fallen tree and were forced to make the first portage.

We hauled our kayaks out of the water and around the downed tree that blocked the river. The smallest of the cypress knees, often hidden just below the surface of the swamp water, constantly hindered our progress pulling the kayaks. Our movement produced first a sucking sound as one foot pulled free of the dark, leaf- and water-covered swamp bottom, then a squishing hiss and splash as we stepped back into the water and mud below it. Our kayaks were relatively light, perhaps 60 pounds each with gear, but they felt heavier with every step of the first portage.

Back on the river, my feet were cold from water that had seeped in when I stumbled in the shallows and found myself up to my knees in the flow across the swamp. The temperature had risen to 55 Fahrenheit but the water felt about 35 as it poured over my boot tops and down and around my toes.

In retrospect, our mindset to the moment of first launch had been one of rather naive good old boys who came from the Lower Little Pee Dee. From a place where the water is wide, the leisurely current manageable with a paddle stroke every now and then. I had foolishly envisioned the river at flood stage as a fast-moving miniature of the dark flow downstream, and of our cutting a swift path between the fallen strainers with an opening always ahead. We needed only be skillful enough in turning our kayaks to master the tricky current that could send us broadside into an obstacle at any moment.

But we were caught up in something different, a tricky, narrow course of swift-flowing water alive with debris, our kayaks little more than two big, bobbing pieces of the relentless movement downstream. Massive limbs and whole trees barred the way in a pattern that resembled the aftermath of a windstorm that had precisely followed the course of the river.

Despite the cool weather sweat formed on my forehead, dripped down my face and soaked my t-shirt underarms. I came alongside Chick and saw water dripping from his brow and his nose. We pumped our paddles, backing up, swinging left and right, constantly seeking the best line, the optimal opening through the limbs and briars and whole trees in the river. In that first half hour we experienced at least a dozen on the edge moments when the kayaks tipped one way or the other, threatening to dump us.

The route down from Red Bluff Lake to County Line Road presents many obstacles including numerous fallen trees that completely block the narrow river channel.

In a backwater opening to the right at a place where the river bent hard left, we gathered ourselves from the initial shock. This was so different from the beautiful, broad river in front of my house at Fork Retch that it was hard to believe the two places were on the same waterway. Five minutes later we pushed on, sliding quickly through the bends, entering close to one bank and coming out of the turns against the other. The end of each turn presented the start of another or revealed a strainer that, if luck was with us, allowed precise left-right movements and a way through. No part of the river thus far had been easy. But things would get better, we reasoned.

In truth, they got worse.

In flood stage the Upper Little Pee Dee turns are breathtaking, sometimes ratcheting us more than 180 degrees at the long bends, sending us back in the general direction of Red Bluff again and again. I would forge ahead and Chick would see me through the swamp growth going in the opposite direction. A few minutes later he would take a cut-through in the swamp and emerge ahead, leaving me to catch sight of him through the foliage going in the opposite direction.

Every bend opened up a new series of obstacles. Limbs and even whole logs rose and fell in the swift flow. Hundreds of roots and limbs waited just below the surface. Our kayaks needed only three inches of water to stay afloat, but we constantly bumped and thumped against the submerged hazards and were thankful for the durability of the sturdy plastic hulls under us. A plywood fishing boat could not make it unscathed down this section at high water without inordinate good luck and an ultra-careful pilot.

We had been on the river about 35 minutes when we reached the State Road 83 Bridge. This fragile-looking wooden trestle crossing is about one third of a mile straight line down from Red Bluff Lake. Quick calculations made it clear that although we were moving briskly from one side of the river to the other and back in the turns, our actual progress downriver was painfully slow. We had at least another eight miles to do and a quick calculation indicated we would not reach the S.C. Highway 57 Bridge before nightfall. We had supplies for an overnight, but Chick needed to be in Columbia the next day, and I wanted to sleep in my own bed that night, not on a bluff above the swamp floor. County Line Road, about three and a quarter miles on the river, looked reachable by late afternoon, so we made the destination change without hesitation.

From the beginning we tried to limit the number of portages. Our first choice was to glide under the fallen trees with limbo-like maneuvers, sliding to the extreme bow of the boat and getting our heads down to the level of the seat back. If we couldn't get under, sometimes there was a way through the branches. That solution was complicated by the fact that many of the trees and practically every stump had a healthy growth of poison ivy. Late winter, as opposed to the rest of the year, offered an advantage in dealing with the overhanging trees and brush. We grabbed branches and pulled them aside far more eagerly than we would have in warm weather, when snakes and wasps were threats.

The last alternative to a portage was the swamp and soon it became our first option when confronted with an obstacle. We quickly became adept at following the fast-moving bubbles around the cypress trunks and those troublesome little knees and back into the river. I leaned forward to hear Chick's comments about a particularly large cypress knee well over six-feet-high and photographed him in its shadow. It was more than 300 years old, he speculated. The Pee Dee Indians who paddled these waters in dugouts saw scenes almost identical to those we were witnessing long before explorers from the Old World appeared, he said.

We paused in another backwater while the river went past swiftly on our left. Even though it was February, some of the red maples, *Acer rubrum*, were starting to bloom and Chick maneuvered his kayak to get a good photograph. A Wood Duck, family *Anitdae*, species *Aix sponsa*, launched into a noisy takeoff as we rounded the next bend and he explained its local wintering habits and differentiated it from *Anas platyrhynchos*, the Mallard, the male of which is distinguished by beautiful green coloring from the neck up.

Such scholarly explanations would be part of our entire river journey since Chick knows the native trees, shrubs and wildlife by common name and the Latin. He can, and often does, conduct a floating lecture, recounting the experiences of countless trips from the South Santee on the Atlantic Coast to the log cabin he built mostly with his own hands in the mountains outside Walhalla in the western corner of the state. I am always duly impressed by the depth of his knowledge.

At the one hour mark, after successfully dodging obstacles and passing over, around and under at least a dozen fallen trees, Chick's kayak hung up on the limb of a submerged oak and the current turned him broadside. Behind me I heard him yell "uh, oh," and when I turned all I could see was the bottom of his 10-foot blue Pungo kayak. It went from a comfortable seat on the river to a long plastic head cover in no more than five seconds.

When he emerged from the water seconds later he was still wearing his hat; he had gotten soaked without wetting his head. He waded ashore with the kayak in tow and changed into a dry shirt stored in the watertight compartment, then stripped out of his warm-up pants into Bermudas although it was probably below 50 degrees.

"Couldn't avoid it," he said. "Once I turned broadside, the current flipped me. At least I kept my hat dry."

"My time is coming," I said. Never had I been more prescient.

Two hours into the paddle, we were still working hard, avoiding the low-hanging branches that reached out from both sides. I remarked that it looked as if the river might be widening slightly.

"Things are looking up," I said.

"I learned in nature to never say things cannot get any worse because they almost invariably do," Chick cautioned.

I didn't respond. But we were through the worst of it, I was sure.

A few minutes after that we came to a classic cut-through where the river had created a new path. The flow was split between the oxbow-shaped channel of water to the left and a swift, narrow stream to the right. An oxbow formation, a familiar feature on the Lumber and the Little Pee Dee, is created when the river meanders wide and then comes back to the original course, creating a U or oxbow-shaped bulge. Gradually the water cuts into the neck of the bulge at its narrowest point and the river flow eventually carves a cut-through across the neck of the oxbow. In high water the flow is both across the neck and around the oxbow. In low water the flow is reduced or cut off completely into the oxbow which collects sandbars at its entrance and exit.

The cut-throughs on the upper river are almost always in the beginning tight openings, sunless little shafts through the vegetation leading to open water somewhere beyond. The water accelerates in the narrow cut, seemingly doubling the speed of the current. I was in the lead and chose the oxbow before it was clear that the main flow was now decidedly coursing into the cut-through. Chick went to the right, through the dark opening, pushing the limbs back as he shot in and quickly came out in the main channel.

Following a swamp cut-through to get around a fallen tree on the Little Pee Dee above County Line Road.

"Come on," he called out. "It's fine. I'm on the other side"

I lined up the bow of my 12-footer for the opening and paddled hard. I almost made it through when my keel hit something under the water with a heavy thump. In two seconds my kayak was broadside to the flow, caught by branches on both sides and lodged on the underwater obstacle amidships. I was almost certainly up against a barely submerged cypress knee. Two or three seconds after that I was upside down with the kayak over my head in the fast moving water. In the darkness I held my camera against my chest with one hand and draped my other arm across the bottom of the overturned kayak. Then I stepped into a hole and went completely under.

"Are you okay?" Chick shouted. "Are you okay?" he called out a second time even louder.

I bobbed up under the kayak and kept repeating one word, "oh, oh, oh" as he shouted his question again and again.

"I thought you were drowning," he told me later.

At that moment, I could not tell him that I was simply reacting to the cold water with the only utterance I could muster. My feet inside my wet socks were already cold from the portages and the swift change from the warmth of the kayak to the jolt of the swift, deep water sent a giant shiver surging from my toes to my scalp. I finally found the bottom sand with my boots and pulled myself to shore using the cypress knees along the bank as handholds. Chick maneuvered his kayak to catch up with my belongings floating in the watertight cockpit cover that had moments earlier been strapped to the kayak.

My digital camera and my mobile phone and lightweight tape recorder had all gotten a good soaking. I did not think any of them would survive in working order. But my wallet, iPhone and car keys had been in the watertight compartment and remained dry. I changed shirts, drained the kayak and pushed it back down to the water. Once back in my seat, I pulled my boots off to drain them and then pushed them back on. Amazingly, my feet were no longer cold and my upper body tingled with warmth.

Minutes earlier, when I was under water struggling to find bottom with the toes of my boots, I had the most extraordinary thought about my friend Albert Finocchiaro, a retired U.S. Army aviator.

"You need to scare yourself to death once a week or life isn't worth living," Albert often reminded me. I didn't follow his advice intentionally but for a few moments under the water in the darkness, with a kayak over my head and the river trying to pull me further under, it occurred to me that Albert would have to give me credit on this day for involuntarily heeding his advice.

We got moving again and even wet and with my camera sidelined because of fried electronics, I felt an internal warmth, a surge like the adrenaline was still flowing. My paddle strokes were powerful and precise. I felt remarkably alive, fortunate to be on this river experience. It had been the kind of moment when my cousin Ben, a Green Beret combat veteran and superb outdoorsman, would have built a roaring fire, brewed coffee and razzed me for capsizing. I was happy and sad and pumped in the same instant, most of all pleased that I had had a good thought of Ben and his brave fight against cancer.

With both of us now properly christened by the Little Pee Dee, it became clear that mastering the first stretch was primarily about endurance and determination, about maneuvering around and over and under the fallen trees; about the delicate balance between risk taking and knowing when to head to shore and portage. The Upper Little Pee Dee provides a measuring stick for how much you really want a real blackwater river experience. In high water, it is clearly a no pain, no gain proposition. The scratches on my face and shins and the bruises I would certainly discover the following day would all be tallied as dues paid for the privilege of riding this river.

Finding a way around the fallen trees, or strainers, was the single most challenging assignment. At high water, many of the downed trees offered a narrow opening through the branches. The best crossing situation came when the tree had fallen completely into the river with a portion of the trunk under water. If there was any flow at all across the trunk we had a good chance of sliding over. As long as we could get the front half of the kayak over it was possible to hop the rest of the craft across and slide down the far side.

The worst thing that could and did happen was to get almost halfway over, then find yourself sitting high and dry on the log. Invariably the heavy stern, where we had our main gear stored in the watertight compartment, would dip down backwards and the current would catch the keel fin and begin to spin the kayak. If you turned, you were going to capsize with the river trying to force you and your craft under the log that barred the way.

The strainers came in pairs and trios and quartets; as soon as we crossed one, another confronted us and another and another. We were forced into quick turns and a constantly evolving plan of how to approach the next opening. The current was moving only four or five miles per hour, just a quick jog on land, but it was amazing how rapidly the decisions had to be made on negotiating turns. Often we hopped our kayaks across a semi-submerged log, then immediately pivoted right or left to head for the best crossing spot of another downed tree and another after that.

We both knew the Chattooga in upper South Carolina, the great whitewater river made famous by James Dickey's novel *Deliverance.* There was, of course, no comparison to the extreme dangers of that white water, but we understood that the Upper Little Pee Dee could drown you just as quickly if you made a mistake. Not once had I ever had that feeling on the lower part of the river.

Chick was able to control his 10-foot kayak in this narrow section of the river better than I maneuvered the 12-footer. But I would still choose my craft if we came back through this stretch. It glided further with fewer strokes and passed through the swamp channels between the cypress knees with less paddling effort. We used standard double-ended kayak paddles, but a single paddle would have been easier to handle in the tight spaces. If we ever repeat the stretch, I will also bring along a short wooden paddle for the swamp work.

I was eventually proven right in saying the river was opening up a bit. Downstream from the cut-through where I capsized the flow slowed and the sandy bottom was only a couple of feet below us. For the first time we passed over stretches of white sand appearing gold colored in the tannin-stained flow.

But we still had to fight our way through the bends. At one turn we chose opposite ends of a strainer. I pushed through the branches at the top end of the fallen tree and came out the other side with a bleeding cheek and minus my favorite South Carolina hat with the palmetto and white crescent emblem. It remained hung up in the briars that had cut me. About the same time, Chick got caught at the other end and nearly turned over. He retreated and came down to the branches where he retrieved my hat on the way through.

We had made our way downriver to a point where the swamp ended on the south bank and a bluff reached perhaps 75 feet above us at its highest point. We now rode the water in what felt like a deep, often dark, miniature river valley, lost in time and in surroundings that would have been familiar to members of the Pee Dee tribe four centuries earlier.

In this section, as we headed straight for a ten-foot bank with the bluff behind it, the river appeared to go left and right. Not until the turn could we see which water was the channel and which was the back eddy that turned into the swamp. I was in the lead on the first of these turns and was fooled by the flow, paddling smartly into the eddy and toward the swamp before realizing my mistake.

Chick warned more than once about poison ivy branches attached to many of the trees leaning out over the water. It poses little threat to you in winter unless you break a branch, he said. That had not been my experience, I told him. I had gotten cases of it often, even in the dead of winter, after inadvertently brushing against leaves growing up trees we were cutting.

I recalled my dad's warning from half a century earlier: "If leaves be three, leave it be." This referred to the three-leaf growth of the plant. *Toxicodendron radicans,* poison ivy, Chick pointed out, has an oily substance called Urushiol, which causes the skin reaction. I wore leather gloves for much of this section and used my paddle to push the undergrowth away when possible.

As noted, the red maples were beginning to bloom and beautiful clumps of fern grew in the riverside bushes along with the poison ivy. Resurrection fern, *Pleopeltis (Polypodium) polypodioides,* usually seen only after a wet spell, sprouted in the high branches of trees over the water.

In early afternoon we saw the first of several large turtles sunning on logs. The temperature had risen to 65 in the direct sunlight.

"If the turtles come out to sun, the cottonmouths will be out also," Chick said. "They like the same temperature."

Somewhere around the four-hour mark, civilization intervened intermittently as we saw the first homes and cabins on the south bluff. At one point we passed the chimneys of what appeared to have once been a farm settlement on the river and saw the lower end of a cultivated field.

The green belt of the Little Pee Dee which is often two miles wide or more on the lower river is by comparison just a sliver of vegetation in the upper stretches. Here the river is centered in a belt sometimes only 300 feet wide.

We arrived at County Line Road, separating Marlboro and Dillon counties, with about three hours of daylight remaining. We were only halfway to the Highway 57 Bridge and had paddled about 4.5 miles on the river. Clearly, we could not have reached our destination before nightfall. As we approached the bridge, a white pickup crossed above us. Moments later it turned and came back.

"Would you give us a ride to our truck?" I called out to the man leaning out the passenger side window above us.

"Sure," he answered. "We wanted to know about your trip anyway."

They parked and came down to the water to give us a hand pulling the kayaks into the bank. They were brothers, fishermen from nearby Dillon. "We retired from a company in Florence and were out on this Friday afternoon just driving around when we saw your kayaks," one said.

"That is the only stretch of the Little Pee Dee I've never paddled down," the other added.

We talked about the strainers and getting dunked. There was more of the same to follow on the next section, they said.

"Did you see Mr. No Shoulders?" the driver asked.

"Sorry," I said, not understanding.

"The cottonmouth moccasin," he said. "We call him Mister No Shoulders around here."

"No, we didn't see him," I answered. "But we started looking after we saw turtles sunning."

They said they had fished the Little Pee Dee from Highway 83 to the Tanyard on the Great Pee Dee. But never the upper section.

When they found out I came from Nichols, they wanted to know if I knew Donald Ray Turner.

"He has the world record for Red Breast," one said. Later I checked and found Turner's 2-pound red breast catch in 1975 in the Lumber River remains the South Carolina record. I told him Turner grew up across the street from the little corner grocery my dad ran in Nichols during the 1950s.

While Chick rode off with the two brothers to get his car I had a sandwich and a diet cola from the dry compartment of the kayak. I laid my wet clothes out in the sun, leaned the paddles up against the kayaks and dozed off with the late afternoon rays bathing my face. There must be something disarming about kayaks because people seem to have no reluctance to stop and find out why you are on the river once they see the kayak. So I was not surprised a few minutes later when the sound of a truck idling a few feet away woke me. The driver was a silver-haired man probably in his eighties. An attractive woman who appeared several years younger sat in the passenger seat. He pulled the Ford 150 pickup across to the wrong side of the road only six feet from me and came to a stop. He turned off the ignition.

"Did you catch any?" he asked.

"We weren't fishing," I said. "Just paddling the river from Red Bluff Lake."

"Did you see any cottonmouths?" he asked.

"Not a one," I said.

"When I was young they were everywhere," he said. "Ain't none of them in the river swamp anymore." The woman beside him looked at me and shook her head as if to say, he doesn't know what he's saying.

"I live up there at the top of the hill." He pointed south in the general direction of Parrish Mill Road.

"Sure you didn't see any snakes?" he asked again. The woman shook her head and I was tempted to say, yes, we ran into a nest of them. But I thought better of it and answered no again. The woman smiled and nodded approval. She turned her head almost constantly, checking in front and behind. Clearly she wanted the conversation to end before someone swept down the hill and hit them.

"No cottonmouths," I said.

"How about reindeer?" he asked. The woman shook her head again.

"Saw some deer up by the McLaurin Pond on Highway 57," I said.

"Alright," he said, and at the woman's urging cranked the truck and drove away.

After he left I pondered his question and that of the two brothers. Are the snakes really that bad along this stretch?

We would be back in warmer weather.

And Mr. No Shoulders would probably be waiting.

County Line Road landing is really just a few feet of cleared area fronting the river on the downstream side of the bridge.

2

Portages And Log Jumps

County Line Road to Highway 57 Bridge (5 Miles)

It was Sunday morning, March 17, when we drove up to the County Line Bridge outside Little Rock north of Dillon. We had tried to get back on the river sooner, but nearly a month had passed since we had taken on the first section of the Little Pee Dee. As we pulled our gear and kayaks down from my truck onto the causeway above the river, we were joined by a fisherman sporting a faded

Carolina Gamecock T-shirt. He slid two small fiberglass boats down the embankment and into the shallow water of a little slough just above the bridge, then came back up to join us. We introduced ourselves and asked him about the fishing and the river.

"There are still some good ones to be caught," he said. "I know the river from here down to the Great Pee Dee, but not much about the upper section. And I have not been on that one from Red Bluff Lake because it is too full of fallen trees." He was Jody Cook, a local fisherman, and he said he would be heading downriver. We wished him luck.

County Line Road in the best of situations does not offer much of a landing, just a few feet of cleared area fronting the river on the downstream side of the bridge. And even that small area was not available when we slid our kayaks down the bank. Someone had cleared brush in the past month and shoved it all alongside the river, covering the best place to launch.

Since the February trip the water had dropped nearly two feet. At the lower level, we would be able to get over fewer logs. But the higher, faster water at flood stage had made turns more treacherous. The slower flow would ease that problem. However, lower water also meant fewer chances to cut through the swamp channels

Local fisherman Jody Cook (l) and author L.L. Gaddy discuss the upper sections of the Little Pee Dee.

Successfully crossing a partially submerged log involves a hard reverse lean on the downhill side after clearing the obstacle.

when confronted by the strainers. With the lower water level we could also see more of the swamp bottom and smell the musty odor of the decaying vegetation.

I wore new boots for the trip, brown leather Herman Survivors that reached to my calf. I like to step into the water and get in the kayak without getting my feet wet. But with the lack of a shallow put-in I stepped in the river up to my knees and the water flowed in and down and around my toes. It was 11 a.m., the outside temperature 73 degrees and the water squishing under my heels almost comfortable, nothing like the cold sensation when we hit the water three weeks earlier. Chick wore his customary open river sandals so he had no such reservations about getting wet. Someone had set out a marker plank on the far side of the bridge with the number five painted as the top numeral on the scale. The water level was perhaps an inch below the five. It had been at approximately seven feet three weeks earlier, we estimated.

The challenge on the approximately four-mile river section down to the S.C. Highway 57 Bridge was clear from the start. The strainers lay across the river from the first turn onward and we knew we would be forced to get over, under or around them for much of the day. How many portages would we have to make and how many log jumps could we execute to avoid hauling our kayaks through the swamp?

A Little Pee Dee log jump is really no jump at all. The secret is to accelerate and get the front half of the kayak across the underwater obstacle and then slide down the other side. Soon after launch I photographed a sequence in which Chick cleared the top of a submerged log, balanced momentarily on the extended fin that begins midway the kayak and then nearly flipped as he leaned to the right and entered the water with the bow heading for the bottom. He overcame the imbalance with a hard reverse lean and slid downward off the log as water washed first over the bow as it hit the water and then the stern as it cleared the log and dipped below the current momentarily.

A temperature range of 65 to 70 degrees Fahrenheit is a sort of magic mark when the snakes and turtles begin to appear in the early season. And over the course of the next four hours we saw a few turtles and several snakes slide into the water at our approach. Chick was disappointed we had seen so few snakes, particularly the cottonmouth moccasin, *Agkistrodon piscivorus*. "In the Congaree Swamp they lie out in the sun and you can get quite close," he said. "Here, they are into the river the moment you round a bend 100 yards away." The absence of snakes somehow reminded Chick of an adventure on the South Santee where he and his son Lin had seen dozens of large alligators. That adventure segued into his report about a paddling trip on Lake Jocassee where he battled strong winds. This morning I was energetically listening to everything Chick had to say. Most of what he talks about is interesting, often fascinating. But when I arrive at information overload, I have an easy way to tune him out for a few minutes. The fact that the hearing in my right ear is not as good as the left enables me to maneuver my kayak in that direction when needed. I never said anything to him about this listening trick, although I suppose he might discover it now.

A couple of bends down the river we came upon the remains of a fishing deck and some steps leading into the water. In the distance on the hill we could see the back of a relatively new, large house. On our previous trip from Red Bluff Lake I met the owner of the house and he had questioned me extensively about whether or not we had seen Mr. No Shoulders, the cottonmouth moccasin. I had hopes we would see the man at the end of the day when I could give him a better report on snake sightings.

The County Line to S.C. Highway 57 Bridge section winds and twists just like the initial run down from Red Bluff Lake. But there is slightly more room to maneuver as the river gradually widens. In the Red Bluff section the channel is often 25 feet or less across. Now it seemed more like 35 feet, sometimes more.

We passed a few fallen trees cut off by a chain saw to clear a way through. But there were also many precariously leaning trees along the bank with eroded roots. All were candidates to fall into the river in the coming months. It seemed impossible to keep the entire path of the river clear all the time.

Thirty minutes downriver we passed the start of a clear cut on the north bank. In most cases, the timber harvest does not come all the way to the riverbank. Loggers leave a couple of mixed rows of large cypresses and oaks. But aerial photos of the entire river show areas where the harvest included nearly everything but a few single trees along the bank. This was one of those cuts with barely a tree at the edge. Beyond that, stumps dotted the swamp floor for as far as we could see.

"They should have left more timber along the river," Chick said. He has a friend in Columbia who is involved in the management of timber for the state and said he would discuss it with him. His inquiry couldn't alter the current logging, but it might prevent such a severe cut elsewhere on the river, he said.

Our first portage came 90 minutes into the trip where a fallen laurel oak completely barred the way. We stopped first for a sandwich and then pulled the kayaks through the swamp mud. For most activities on the river, it's really best to wear lightweight shoes, or even open rubber sandals like Chick's. However, I am partial to shin-high boots and they paid off during this portage as we stepped over and around cypress knees, the above ground roots of the cypress forest. On the water our technique steadily improved as we continued to slide across the logs. By the fourth crossing of a log barely below the surface of the water we were going over with speed, counterbalancing as the kayak teetered atop the log momentarily on the keel and then inevitably counter leaning to one side or the other on the downward slide. Without using this technique we would have had at least four more portages.

At a bend in the river we came upon a medium-sized oak that had fallen years before. It survived and now grew diagonally out over the river, reaching at least 25 feet across the channel. The big tree's limbs had developed into half a dozen small oaks in their own right, each pointing to the sky from the main trunk.

It was 3:30 when we saw the Highway 57 Bridge and moments later entered the little slough where Jody Cook had slid his boats down that morning. We had been on the water for five and a half hours and covered barely five miles. Behind us were the two sections locals said were the hardest on the river.

But more than 100 miles of paddling still remained.

Good flexibility is required crossing under a fallen tree downriver from the Highway 57 Bridge Landing.

3

Beware Of Tame Ducks

Highway 57 Bridge to McKays Bridge (5 Miles)

At our starting point, S.C. Highway 57 Bridge, we slid our kayaks down the narrow incline to the little slough-like indention in the river where we had come ashore three weeks earlier. The river was higher, up two feet from our last paddle, almost at the depth we had experienced on the opening section from Red Bluff Lake. The weather was good, sunny, a high of 75 predicted. It was Sunday April 7.

This stretch measured 2.88 miles in a straight line on Google Earth and we estimated the actual length would be about five miles, depending on how many swamp detours we took to avoid strainers. The flow was brisk and it took us quickly under a canopy of green. Ten minutes downriver a fallen live oak blocked the entire river. But we scooted around it neatly in a narrow swamp channel no more than six inches deep and exited fifty feet downriver.

The temperature climbed through the sixties and into the low seventies as noon passed and then one p.m. We did not see a snake until a moccasin dropped from a stump beside the river after Chick floated by and just as I came alongside. The snake startled me and I did a little jump as if I were lifting the kayak across a log. I didn't see the snake again but pulled hard on my paddle a couple of times to get clear of that particular piece of water.

Chick likes observing snakes and seeks them out. In 40 years of walking the outdoors he has had many close calls with all kinds of poisonous snakes but has never been bitten. He does not kill snakes of any kind. I once saw a snake crawling up the wall of his log cabin in Walhalla and asked about it. It was a black snake, he said, and he was letting it sleep in his attic for the winter.

The snake in question had been Blackie, a pet that his son Lin had known as a child. At that time neither he nor Chick would kill any living creature in their home. That has not changed. A few months ago Chick told me another black snake is living somewhere in his cabin. He found the snake's shed skin on his kitchen countertop this past spring. "The field mice come in when I'm gone," he said, "and the snake kills them."

I have also never been bitten and likewise have had a number of close calls. But I have no hesitation in killing a poisonous snake if it is near where I live, work or play. My cousins Ben and Gene always put me in the back of the boat as the paddler when we went hunting for bullfrogs at night. Gene sat in the front with a rifle and a flashlight while Ben was in the middle holding a long pole with a three-pronged gig mounted on the end. I paddled in the dark, following the path of Gene's flashlight. One night I swept the paddle behind me and was convinced I hit something alive moving in the water. Gene shone the light onto our wake and said we were being followed by a cottonmouth. He stood and shot several times over my shoulder, killing the snake, he said. Gene was a lifelong jokester so I wasn't sure there had even been a snake behind us, but spent the rest of the night sweeping my paddle vigorously behind the boat at the end of each stroke. The snake dropping in the water beside me brought back memories of that night on the pond with my cousins and I vowed to stay a little further from the overhanging limbs where the snakes often sunned.

There were few branches or limbs on the cutover north bank of this section. The clear cut that we had seen on our last trip continued. Mostly there were only single trees on that side of the river, many of them good candidates to fall in and eventually denude the bank of big trees.

"Did you find out who monitors the cutting?" I asked.

"The real answer appears to be no one," Chick said.

On one bend, in a clear cut of perhaps 50 acres, a single, massive cypress remained standing about 300 feet from the riverbank.

"The top is broken out and it looks hollow," Chick said. "That's probably why they left it."

Half an hour into the paddle, the clear cut ended and we once again entered swamp forest, passing between big cypresses mostly mixed with oaks and red maples. We could see stands of mature loblolly pines further inland.

The turns in this third stretch were again acute. Over and over one of us would see the other through the trees, reversing direction. But we weren't as rushed in making the turns and lining up for the best angle to get past the next strainer. Either we were getting better or the river was now less formidable. Or both.

The water in the swamp was still deep enough to get us past nearly all the strainers and complete blockages of the channel. Chick talked about the sinuosity of the river, an index used to measure how much a river twists and turns. He suggested a rolling index for the Little Pee Dee in which the upper river might be nearly three times the measured straight line distance. The lower river, past the confluence with the Lumber, might only be two times as long as the straight line measurement or even less than the factor of two, he speculated.

We saw few homes, cabins or signs of former settlement such as old chimneys or rotting docks as we made our way down this stretch of river. Over the course of the paddle we came alongside perhaps half a dozen places where signs of civilization interrupted nature along the bank. There is, of course, plenty of debris on the upper river. Even along a route characterized by dark, haunting, natural beauty, there is, however, occasional, extreme ugliness. Trash clogs countless eddies against fallen trees. Beer cans, lawn chairs, rotting tires, the hulls of old boats and clothing articles of every kind and color float in filthy scum foam as a harsh reminder of how little some among us feel the responsibility to preserve the river for those who come after.[2] In fairness I should add that my college friend Charlie Bethea of Marion, a board member of the Pee Dee Land Trust, says the water quality and general cleanliness of the river is much improved from two decades earlier and continues to get better.[3]

Again we saw signs that someone with a chain saw had been at work trying to clear away the worst of the strainers, opening a way for adventurous boaters. In the first section nothing had been done to clear the river. In the second some of the worst of the log barriers had been cut. Upon reflection, I think it better that the upper river remain natural. The harder it is to make the paddle, the more satisfaction in the accomplishment. There are plenty of stretches later along the 27-mile natural scenic river section in Dillon County that can and should be cleared for casual paddlers.

At the end of the first hour we paused in front of a rusted out house trailer parked on a high bank on the north side of the river. The owner had once had a dock down on the river, but it had long ago broken away and all that remained were a few rotting support pilings. The structures constructed on the river—docks, fishing benches, even huts at the waterside—are apparently never cleaned up and cleared away when they begin to fall apart. Everything is left to rot and the rot eventually falls into the river and joins the rest of the trash.

Ninety minutes into the trip a slim, 40-foot long water oak blocked the river completely. We retreated upstream and Chick found a narrow swamp flow only about six inches deep but moving swiftly. His 10-footer made it through easily. I hung up a couple of times unable to negotiate the same tight turns in my 12-footer. Finally I came through also. Despite the high water, the sandbars had begun to emerge on the inside of turns. In another month the white sand, now gold colored in appearance under a few inches of dark water, would begin to shimmer in a hundred places along this stretch.

We broke for lunch two and a half hours into the trip, stopping on a grassy bank at the end of a fire break in a pine forest that reached almost to the river bank. There were no sounds save   birds chirping, the up and down splashing of a log bobbing in the water nearby and the rustling of tree boughs stirred by a light wind.

Tame Muscovy ducks patrol the river bank near a home between the Highway 57 Bridge and McKays Bridge.

Just below our lunchtime stop a sign warned: Beware of Tame Ducks. Moments later we passed ten feet from two Muscovy ducks watching us warily on the bank. These unusual looking ducks, with telltale red patches around the eyes and near iridescent green-black wing feathers, are more common in the Lower Rio

Grande Valley of Texas and Mexico. Chick ventured a guess we were seeing *Cairina moschata domestica*, the tame version of the Muscovy. Males can reach 15 pounds and these ducks had obviously adapted to the colder weather along the river compared to the higher Southwest and Central American temperatures.

A screened deck on the river and a house were the first buildings we saw on the paddle. In short order we saw another cabin, a second house and a house trailer. When we rounded the first bend past the tame duck warning, another sign about the ducks was posted on a riverside deck and pier. A "No Trespassing" sign barred entry to a screened room on a deck above the water. A Mallard swam lazily behind a rope that cut off entry to the shore fronting the buildings. These houses, the remains of a trailer and a lone chimney turned out to be the only dwellings seen on the stretch.

Ninety minutes after the lunch stop we arrived at McKays Bridge, five miles downriver. There had been no obvious spot to take out our kayaks when we stopped to leave Chick's car four and a half hours earlier. A diving tower nailed high on a tree showed that the north bank, where the current had apparently cut a deep hole along the bank, was not a good candidate. A few moments later Chick found a narrow shelf a few feet further down the bend where we could come ashore in six inches of water.

We climbed the high bank to the road and met David and Denise Cochran and their sons Makoa and Ikaika fishing from the bridge. They weren't catching anything but the visit seemed more about family time than fishing. Denise said she was originally from Hawaii. David said he was a local who now runs a nearby transmission repair shop.

We left them baiting hooks for the boys and enjoying the river.

Local residents David and Denise Cochran and sons Makoa and Ikaika take a break from fishing near McKays Bridge.

Metal collector Tommy Branch tells the story of the cross commemorating the life of Michelle Brown.

4

A Cross For Michelle Brown

McKays Bridge to Harllees Bridge (7 Miles)

The sun was up but the thermometer under 60 when we reached Harllees Bridge, a short drive from the crossroads town of Little Rock on S.C. Highway 9 a few miles outside Dillon. Today's high was going to be in the sixties, unusually cool weather for the third week of April when the morning temperature should have already been in the 70's and climbing.

Our plan was to leave Chick's car and immediately drive up to McKays Bridge, but a white wooden cross alongside the steep road down to the river bank at Harllees Bridge caught our attention as we parked his car. The horizontal piece, two 2x4's nailed together and buried in the ground, had written in dark lettering 'Baby Sister Michelle Brown.' The mortised transverse of the cross bore the inscriptions 5/18/1972 and 12/11/2010. Grass and weeds grew up around a bouquet of withered flowers placed at the foot of the cross.

Up the hill, a few hundred yards away, a man slowly walked toward us along the grassy road shoulder. He carried a pick up tool in one hand and a plastic bucket in the other. As he walked he methodically retrieved metal cans from the roadside with the tool and dropped them in the bucket.

Tommy Branch introduced himself. "I live a few miles away," he said. "I had a heart attack and my doctor told me to walk. So I'm out here picking up aluminum."

What about the cross?

"About three years ago a woman parked down near the water," he said. "Her car drove into the water. She drowned." He showed us the path the car took into the water.

Later I checked online and found the following obituary in the Dillon Herald from December 13, 2010. It noted: "Services for Michelle Lee Brown will be held Wednesday at 4 P.M. in Cooper Funeral Home Chapel with burial at Mt. Zion Baptist Church Cemetery."[4]

Branch said he had done some fishing on the river but had not explored the upper section. We exchanged addresses and he continued on his way, looking for more metal.

We drove back up to McKays Bridge with both kayaks in the truck bed and found the same parking spot on the north side of the bridge we used two weeks earlier. The water level had fallen about ten inches since the last outing. For a change, I kept my feet dry getting into the kayak. A little victory for the new boots that proved themselves waterproof as long as the water didn't come in over the top. As always, Chick wore his open river sandals and waded in without hesitation. The map showed four miles straight-line to Harllees Bridge. We estimated the trip would be seven miles on the river. The Trimble trekking app on Chick's iPhone showed we would have at least two long, almost straight stretches where we could make good time.

Our expectations were primed for a day of light paddling with no need to get out of the kayaks except for breaks. But that thought disintegrated as we rounded the first bend. A fifty-foot oak had fallen into the river, blocking the narrow channel and a big broken limb lay atop the tree trunk at a point where perhaps an inch of water flowed across. Chick edged up to the barrier and found it passable if the limb could be removed. He pushed and prodded for a couple of minutes with his paddle, careful not to damage the plastic blades. He worked the big limb from several angles, avoiding the trap of getting side on to the fallen oak and then being flipped by the power of the current. Finally the limb broke free, floating downstream and out of sight in moments.

"I'm going across," Chick said, then back paddled hard to get about ten feet of distance between his kayak and the log. He made his run directly at the fallen tree at the point where the river barely flowed across a narrow section of the trunk. His 10-footer hit with a loud thump followed by a muffled scraping sound and a second later he splashed across on the far side.

I didn't have enough speed when I crossed and stalled on top of the submerged tree. Only a few minutes into the trip I found myself on the verge of another dunking. I knew what had to be done and set to work hopping the kayak over, lifting up and leaning forward, while maintaining balance so I didn't fall off to either side. I moved a few inches, then another half a foot and finally the stern came out of the water and I was headed down into the dark current on the far side. The bow went under momentarily and water splashed around me and onto the camera in my lap. But just as quickly the front end of the 12-footer popped up and I was floating again.

In the first quarter hour we faced three more fallen trees blocking the channel. Two of them offered a sliding, straight-on crossing at the low end and we successfully mastered both challenges with definitive thumps and scraping as we went over. The third fallen tree barrier was completely above the level of the water with no place to go over or under. We retraced our route upriver and found the most promising of the swamp channels, one barely the width of the kayaks. We banged and bumped between the cypress knees for the next five minutes, finally emerging into the main channel a bend downstream from the big tree that had barred our way. Not long afterwards the river opened up. Temporarily. It was perhaps 20 feet wider on average and the bends slightly less serpentine. From there on we were able to maintain our speed, sliding by the fallen trees left and right without hard maneuvering. We probably were traveling 2.5 to 3 miles per hour, a superb pace on the Upper Little Pee Dee.

We stopped after 90 minutes just above two houses built alongside the river. We had seen them on Google Earth at the end of a dirt road called Hidden House Place. The older structure seemed a bit neglected but the second house had a fine screen porch visible from the river side and a brick facade on the other side. A check of the map showed three-tenths of our planned trip was behind us and we were slightly ahead of our planned pace.

For the first two hours we heard the throaty roar of a big diesel engine. And as we rounded a gentle bend we saw the first sign of a timber clear cut behind the two or three remaining rows of trees and knew another section of the north side was being chopped. The entire forest had been taken down for as far as we could see, and the clear cut signaled by the sound of the big engine continued for another mile on the river although we never saw the men or the machines doing the cutting.

We took a second break ninety minutes later at an unmarked landing with a dirt road leading away from the river into a pine forest. Our best estimate was that we were about half a mile from Oakland Road leading toward the North Carolina line. A Tiger Swallowtail, *Papilio glaucus*, the state butterfly of South Carolina, joined us for this snack. The butterfly spent a lot of time on the ground between the kayaks where a riverbank campfire had once burned. The yellow and black winged swallowtail was attracted to the charcoal remains of the fire, Chick explained.

Twice during the morning we took intentional detours into dead arms of the river and oxbows so Chick could explore the plant life. The oxbows in high water are navigable, functioning channels of the river. Birds often retreat into the oxbows and you are likely to find a Great Blue Heron, *Ardea herodias,* fishing the shallows. If we spot an alligator on this upper section of the river, we know it will probably be in an oxbow, usually the quietest and most private place on the river. Later in the year, when sandbars build up at both entrance and exit, the fish that remain will be trapped until high water returns or they suffocate for lack of oxygen in the water.

There are alligators this far upriver, residents say, but neither of us has ever seen one above the junction with the Lumber River at Fork Retch. A half century earlier there weren't many sightings this far from the coast. But that has changed. The state alligator population, once endangered, grew to over 100,000 by the year 2000. Record alligators have been killed in the state's two largest lakes, Marion and Moultrie, both created in the 1939-1942 Santee-Cooper hydroelectric project. A 13-foot alligator shot in Lake Marion in October of 2009 weighed 1,060 pounds.

Once we reach The Retch, we'll keep a sharper lookout. Gators up to six feet have been sighted between there and the S.C. Highway 917 Bridge at Sandy Bluff Landing. In recent years there have also been black bear sightings along the river, marking the comeback of this rarely-seen mammal in our part of the country. Common wisdom is that neither the alligators nor the bears on the river want anything to do with humans and shy away at the first sight of boaters. But a 13-foot gator, with jaws wide enough to take down a wild pig or deer or crack open a 12-foot kayak, really fears nothing.

Between McKays Bridge and Harllees Bridge, several creeks drain the swamp and it is possible to paddle miles into the trees along the creeks at high water. A South Carolina Department of Natural Resources guide on the river notes, "This 8-mile section of the river…is also very remote and swampy with narrow channels. There are many opportunities to get lost exploring multiple channels within the floodplain at higher water levels. One may want to enter this section at the break of dawn as it can take an entire long summer day to complete. Travel at any water level can be very difficult and is recommended for the experienced boater only."[5] The DNR publication probably errs on the side of caution. Clearly, even at low water, it would not take all day to cover the stretch.

Uprooted trees often bar direct downriver passage on the upper Little Pee Dee.

On a couple of occasions the main river and the oxbow flow were about equally divided. The Upper Little Pee Dee is so sinuous that you can almost always see the next turn through the swamp. It already appeared that once beyond the difficult first two sections, as long as you are careful, avoid the poison ivy and stay in the main channel, you can methodically and relatively easily work your way down. Portages during low water will add to your time on the river, however.

On this day we saw water snakes but no moccasins, Chick's favorites. He knows them well from his life's work and from research for his book on the Congaree Swamp. They should be sunning today, he predicted. But as we reached each likely resting spot, it was empty. Moments after we rounded a bend, most of the snakes either dropped into the water with a loud splash, or slid off their log perches quietly. There were more turtles. They usually waited until we got within fifty feet to drop off the log or limb on which they were sunning. The biggest of them were the large soft-shelled variety which looked to be more than two feet in length including its exceptionally long neck and a tail.

We saw birds in great numbers for the first time on the upper river. Perhaps they had been absent for the winter, or had just flown away at our approach. But beginning with the first minutes on the river this day we shared the swamp with many Wood ducks, Mallards and Canada geese and an occasional Great Blue Heron.

The liftoff of a Great Blue is impressive. It rises from the water effortlessly thanks to wings that span nearly seven feet. Its yellow legs dangle initially and it pulls its long neck back into a tight S shape during flight. When startled the Great Blue usually flies a few hundred yards downriver and begins to fish again. This pattern was repeated four or five times by the first Great Blue we encountered. Each time we rounded a bend and came into sight, it lifted off and set down around the next bend, apparently never considering that a double back would have eliminated our presence for good.

A Red-shouldered Hawk, *Buteo lineatus*, followed us from above for several minutes. We had probably disturbed a hunt. In early afternoon an owl flew out of the trees above the river and disappeared over the clear cut. We heard a large animal in the swamp, most likely a deer or a feral hog. Two Turkey Vultures circled the sky lazily above the clear cut. And somewhere in the distance a Barred Owl, *Strix varia*, called out, *who, who—who, who, who*. Chick cupped his hands to his mouth and mimicked the call.

After five hours on the river, about 4 p.m., we heard roadway traffic and a few minutes later saw the remains of concrete steps leading down to the river on the south side of Harllees Bridge. The location, popular as a swimming hole in the early 1900's, is now overgrown. The best landing was on the downstream side of the bridge at the spot where the man we met earlier, Tommy Branch, had told us the story of the car that went into the water in 2010.

The area just above Harllees Bridge in the distance was a popular swimming place on the river more than a century earlier.

If not for the fallen trees that block the channel on many bends in the section, the 7.25-mile run from McKays to Harllees would be an excellent starting section for paddlers to begin exploration of the Upper Little Pee Dee. It requires a minimum of boating expertise to navigate the stretch and the outstanding scenery rivals that from the headwaters at Red Bluff Lake.

We did the usual shuffle of my driving up in Chick's car to get the truck, then returning to get us both packed up. Then back up the river to get his car and load his kayak again. After that, on the way out, we stopped at the historical road marker beside Saint Paul's Methodist Church on Harllees Bridge Road, two blocks from the S.C. Highway 9 intersection in the settlement of Little Rock.

The marker notes: "This church was established prior to 1803 and was known as Liberty Chapel. The present structure, built in 1871, is significant both for its architecture and as a reflection of Methodism in the Pee Dee area. A Victorian adaptation of the classic meeting-house form. St. Paul's was entered in the National Register of Historic Places in 1977."[6]

St. Paul's Methodist Church on Harllees Bridge Road at Little Rock is on the National Register of Historic Places.

James Caulder, a retired U.S. Army First Sergeant, headed the Pee Dee Indian Tribe for nine years ending in late 2013.

5

Chief James Caulder And The Pee Dee Indian Tribe

When Spanish explorer Juan Pardo came to what is now the South Carolina coast in the 1560s he reported encountering a native people called the *Vehidi,* pronounced Ve-ee-dee and later Pee Dee. "The tribe was listed by the English in the 1740s as one of the 22 nations forming the Catawba Nation, but later identified them as Creek, Essau, and Cherokee Indians," the Pee Dee tribal history notes.[7] Today, the Pee Dee Indian Tribe of South Carolina, which once had a population numbering in the thousands, officially has about 300 members. But in Dillon and Marlboro County, S.C., and in the bordering areas of

North Carolina there are perhaps another 2,000 individuals who qualify for tribal membership.

The tribe headquarters is at McColl, S.C., and the chief until late 2013 was James Caulder, a retired U.S. Army First Sergeant who spent much of his working time the past eight years keeping the heritage of his ancestors alive. The Pee Dees are recognized as an official Indian tribe by the State of South Carolina but not by the U.S. government. Federal recognition has been pending for 20 years and Caulder, 74, said "I don't think I will see that recognition in my lifetime."[8]

The tribe, which gave its name to the area's two primary rivers and to the Pee Dee Region, was present at the beginning as English settlers landed on the coast and moved inland, eventually displacing the multiple tribes that had once been the primary settlers. Members of the Pee Dee tribe fought alongside English colonists in 1711 in the Tuscarora War and in 1715-1717 during the Yemassee War. Illnesses borne by the European settlers threatened extinction of the tribe in the following decades. The tribal history notes, "From the early 1800s until the Civil War of 1861-1865 the descendants of the Original Pee Dee Indians had become small family clans that lived on the rivers and also some were sharecroppers for the white farmers that were the descendants of the settlers that were helped by the Pee Dee Indians to defeat the Red Coats and a host of other Indian tribes all the way down to Florida. The Pee Dee Indians fought in the Civil War and there are many tribal members that trace their Indian Heritage back to those Soldiers."[9]

"I have three Indian bloodlines," Caulder said. My mother Mattie was Cherokee. And my father was Pee Dee and Cheraw. Those three combinations, how they came together, that's another story. But now my great great grandfather, Ananias Noah Caulder. He was a white man. He was Welsh. That's where I get these grey green blue eyes from."

Caulder's great grandfather, Ananias Noah Caulder Jr., fought for the South in the Civil War. "In the oral history that was passed down from my grandfather to my father," Caulder said, "the story goes that Ananias met an Indian maiden up in the Society Hill area on the Great Pee Dee.

"Now you know there is a Welsh Neck settlement up there. Supposedly he met this Indian maiden up there. And she was Pee Dee. But also, she was mixed with the Cheraw. That started the Indian connection with the Welsh ancestors. But from that time forward, the next one in line was my great great grandfather Noah married back into the Indians. That has continued down to me. The next one was my great grandfather. He was Ananias Noah Caulder Jr., and he fought for the South in the Civil War. And I had two or three more uncles in the Civil War. My grandfather Alf was born in 1869, four years after the surrender of the South. And he did not like Yankees. And I imagine he got that, when he grew up you had the Carpetbaggers and everything else in this area down here. When the Yankees came in, any hogs, any food that they had, they took it all. And left them with nothing. I know my grandfather did not own slaves but he was in the Civil War. As far as I know from the history, they didn't own land except for the little bit they was camping on.

"My father was Eddie Caulder. My mother was a Cherokee. She was a Jackson. And her history goes back to the Indians up in the mountains. She told me she was from the Wolf clan of the Cherokee nation."

Caulder said that in 1757 the major settlement of the Pee Dee tribe was located along the current Florence County-Marion County line at what is now Pee Dee, S.C. "Eventually the tribal members migrated from the Winyah Bay all the way into Town Creek near Mt. Gilead, N.C.," Caulder said.[10] "We were connected with the Waccamaws, the Santees, the Edisto. All the Indians that lived along the rivers."

"Our people lived in between the two Pee Dee Rivers," Caulder added. "They had areas along the rivers that were cleaned out every year and they would plant squash, they would plant beans, they would plant corn. And they used the rivers for fishing and hunting. They used fish traps. My daddy made those traps using the willow bark. He would take that willow bark and let it dry out. Then he would weave it into a basket. There was a little opening in the front and the fish would swim in. But they didn't have sense enough to swim out."

The tribe would herd deer into shallows and club them. "Every bit of the deer was used," he said. "For bears…they would dig a hole, then cover it. When the bear went to the bait, it would fall in the hole. Then they would kill it with the lances once it was trapped. In this area hundreds of years ago, there were still some American Bison. I don't have any oral history on how they hunted the Bison. But for the deer I know they did have bows and they had lances."[11]

Caulder was born near the Little Pee Dee headwaters at Red Bluff in 1939. "As a kid I remember us carrying corn to the Red Bluff grist mill there," he said. "And there used to be a power plant, a generator that fed the electricity to Clio. We used to walk the bank, both sides, down from Red Bluff. In those days, with a little wooden boat, we could go all the way down through there without a whole lot of trouble except when we'd have storms. After that we would go down through there and cut those trees out. When I left to go into the military back in the sixties, it was still usable. We still fished it. But today, it's all grown up."

He learned from his father to fish in the swiftest turns of the river. "We'd take a cane pole, one we had cut from along the bank, with a line and some sinkers on it, and an earthworm," Caulder said. "Stick it in the bank, especially in early April and May. The fish we caught, we called them the Red Breasts, Red Breast robins. My tackle box in those days was a Prince Albert tobacco can. Sinkers, hooks and my corks. The corks that I used, they came out of liquor bottles."

The Pee Dees traveled the river in dugouts made from cedar and pine, Caulder said. "According to my grandfather they would pick out a big round tree," he said. "They did not have saws to cut it down. The way they got it down was to make a mud pack up above the base of the tree. Then they would build a fire and burn the tree down. And they would burn off on the other end. They would use stone tools to shave it until they could get the bottom flat. And then they would do the same thing to the top and then would burn it out.

"The tribe had paths all along the river and through the countryside. They would walk from what is now Dillon to Latta to Clio. And to Society Hill near the Great Pee Dee. There were paths up into North Carolina and into the mountains. In Marion County, there was two trails. Liberty Street in Marion, S.C., was originally part of a trail that went all the way up into North Carolina, all the way up to Fayetteville. The other was a Northern trail that run up to the mountains. There was a crossroads at Marion with the Indians from the Southern part of Georgia, or Georgia and Florida migrating north toward New York. It was a kind of corridor. Marlboro County was kind of like an upper end of it. That's why you find now a lot of Indians that's in the area of Dillon County, Marion County and Marlboro County and right on back down into the edge of Georgia.

"Grandfather said anytime they got lost they would look at the sun and they knew if they would follow the sun east or west they would end up at one of the two rivers. I was always told that if I got lost, the first thing I was to do was stop and not panic. Then look for higher ground. If I could see a pine tree, go to the pine tree because pine trees didn't grow in the water."

Caulder said he feels the strongest connection to his ancestors when he is on the river. "I got a modern boat with a 20 horsepower motor behind it," he said. "But I will turn everything off and drift. I can feel the sense of my ancestors, the spirits of my ancestors. In my mind's eye I can look back in time and see along that river."

He remembers hearing the Cherokee language when he was a boy. "My mother could speak Cherokee," he said. "But she would not allow me or my two sisters to learn Cherokee. And the reason, according to her, now I can understand, back then I didn't, was that you have to learn to live in the white man's world. We're talking about when my oldest sister was born in 1930, about a time frame when it was not cool to be Indian at all. So you denied the Indian heritage to survive outside. But you maintained that heritage within the family unit. When I went out in the community the community didn't want to accept me as Indian. That's why I didn't go to school until I was 10 years old." He said the state of South Carolina itself tried to eliminate the Indian race and "create nothing but black and white races. An Indian wasn't worth anything. You couldn't get tax off an Indian."

"Our tribe did not live in teepees," Caulder said. "Now my mother said that her mother told her that the Cherokees, like the Pee Dees, were living in wooden houses or stick built houses, made like little round houses or huts. But then in the 1700s they began to build cabins like the white man. They were trying to become assimilated, to live like the white man."

Caulder quit school after the 4th grade at age 13. Four years later he joined the Army where he earned his high school equivalency diploma. He retired in 1985 as a Senior Non-Commissioned Officer with more than 24 years' service including 18 months in Vietnam with the 4th Infantry Division during the worst of the fighting in 1968-1969. Since his retirement he has become an ordained minister with the First Nation Church of Tulsa, Ok., and a Methodist lay minister. He became chief in 2004.

"My ancestors believed, and I believe today, in a creator God," Caulder said. "We've got one God. It doesn't matter whether he's Yahweh, the Great I AM, Quaker-Hun-te. Whatever you want to call him, he's that one spirit.

"I believe when I close my eyes in this life my spirit goes back where it came from. And that spirit is out there mingled with all the other thousands and millions of Indian spirits that's been there for eons. When I ride the Little Pee Dee, or just look at a wood line, I'll think to myself, was my great grandfather here? Was my great grandmother here? And I feel connected to everything around me. When I go in the woods I'm connected. I see animals and I'm connected to them. I'm not afraid of animals, I'm not afraid of dogs. I have a connection to them. I'm not afraid of snakes. I respect snakes. I'll catch them, but I got to make sure I know how to get ahold of them. My mother was a Cherokee and her belief from her ancestors was that they were always here. That's why they were known as the principal people. They believed that the creator made them and put them in this part of the world. And that creator they referred to as The Great Spirit. Now the Pee Dees worshipped one God or one Supreme Being, but they were connected to everything around. They believed that the snakes were our cousins, that the creatures were our cousins, even the little bugs were connected to us and they honored that.

"That's why we call it Mother Earth. We call Grandfather Sky. And Grandmother Moon. If you notice in here in these four corners of my office, you'll see four different colors. You'll see a white corner over here for the north, a black corner for the west, red corner for the south, and a yellow corner for the east. We believe in these four directions, from which the four winds come and honor the guardians of those spirits that brought those winds.

"My people believed that everything was created by one Supreme Being and he had the spirits that was with him and all the spirits that leave here go back. And somewhere in time these spirits come again, not reincarnation. But these spirits mingle back in. How else can I explain the feeling like I've been here before?"

The paddle from Harllees Bridge to Stafford's Bridge begins with an easy uncomplicated six-tenths of a mile straight stretch.

6

What Noise?

Harllees Bridge to Stafford's Bridge (7.5 Miles)

At Harllees Bridge outside Little Rock, the water level had dropped at least two feet since our visit three weeks earlier. It was mid-May, the temperature warm and the forecast good for our nearly eight-mile trip to Stafford's Bridge on U.S. Highway 301 at Dillon. We pushed off before eleven and found the initial stretch wide and the flow almost non-existent. The river barely moved. This uncomplicated stretch continued for about six–tenths of a mile during which we made excellent progress by pulling hard on our paddles.

At that point the river branched left and right. The left channel led into an open swamp flat, heavy with alligator weed and that way would probably have gotten us back to the river near the end of a lake like arm of the river we planned to visit. But we chose the right channel as the surer bet and proceeded to twist and turn downriver with lowland forest on the south bank and clear cut on the north.

The lower river level had exposed more logs and the branches and trunks of additional fallen trees in the water. Passage was complicated again, but we were able to bump along at a steady pace, sliding across many underwater obstacles without damage. Almost a mile downriver, we reached the mouth of the largest open body of water on this stretch of river. It is directly behind Little Rock on the north bank and would turn out to be the largest lake like formation on the entire Upper Little Pee Dee; it probably had been a stretch of the river cut off by the meandering flow through the flood plain. Had we earlier taken the left branch and successfully worked our way through the swamp, we would have emerged at the north end of the water we dubbed Big Arm Lake.

Large is a relative term in this case, since the water in Big Arm measured about 800 feet long by 120-feet wide. The width narrowed to only about 40 feet at the entry to the swamp. Half a dozen small channels can be seen from aerial photos running through the clear cut swamp floor. Once we were well into the lake, fish began to break the water consistently as we moved up the middle. These were most likely Bowfin (*Amia calva*), locally called Mudfish or simply Muds. They have a habit of breaking the water and gulping air. Mudfish tend to multiply quickly and eventually dominate the fish culture in these small lakes.

From time to time on the Lower Little Pee Dee I have intentionally angled for Mudfish from my kayak and a 10-pounder will twirl your craft and pull it across the water. A Mudfish filet is cottony and not particularly tasty. But the fight to land one on light tackle is worth the effort. At the end of Big Arm we could see a wide expanse of alligator weed and more water. There was a big clear-cut area visible to the northwest and probably enough water there to partially explore. But we took a few photographs and saved that area for a look when higher water levels would guarantee transit all the way across.

From Big Arm Lake we paddled another 45 minutes through classic, uncut swamp forest, passing Norton's Landing on the south bank, then a line of upscale homes on the north bank off Roy Lee Road. They are reached from Oakland Road outside the rural settlement of Hamer northeast of Dillon. A short distance below the houses we found the rotting pilings of a narrow bridge that once spanned the river, perhaps a century earlier. It was not clear if it had been purpose-built for logging traffic or as a crossing for people and livestock. The pilings are so numerous and dangerous that extreme caution must be exercised in times of high water when the jagged creosote stumps are below the surface.

Moccasin Bluff Landing, our lunch stop, was another mile and a half easy paddling downriver. The Little Pee Dee runs for 48 miles in Dillon County, the first 21 from County Line Road and the remaining 27 from Moccasin Bluff. The latter section, from Moccasin Bluff to the Highway 41 Bridge between Fork and Lake View, is the Little Pee Dee Scenic River Water Trail. We spread our sandwiches on a towel and lunched on the ground at Moccasin Bluff. It was our halfway point for the day and the most scenic landing we had encountered thus far. Shade trees provided picnic spots. And the parking lot could easily accommodate 100 cars. The landing is a good one, but the oxbow was so silted up the landing was already unsuited for all but the smallest boats. In low water it would probably be completely dry.

When we pushed off after lunch we knew we had two miles or more to go through dense swampland, all of it behind the Dillon Speedway and Dillon Airport near Interstate 95. There is disagreeable news about this section for the paddler who takes to the river for serenity. Road noise is considerable, an annoying rumble that increases with every bend on the way to I-95. The noise began almost as soon as we pushed away from Harllees Bridge. It began as a faint rumble and became increasingly louder with each successive bend downriver until there was no mistaking the vehicle sounds of Interstate 95. By the time we sighted the I-95 Bridge at the five mile mark on the trip, the noise approached the level of low grade thunder.

Accept the fact that nothing will abate the noise of the interstate without earplugs or headphones canceling out normal hearing. And if that were not enough, as soon as we saw the I-95 Bridge, the vehicle noise climbed another notch because the traffic rolling through the swamp two miles downriver at the U.S. 301 Bridge also announced itself.

Before we could pass under the I-95 Bridge we were forced to portage. A massive laurel oak blocked the entire river at perhaps its widest point all day. We put in on the north bank in water about two feet deep and dragged the kayaks between cypress knees to get around the oak. The mud along the bank was eight to ten inches deep and our feet sank to ankle depth with each step.

Chick got his kayak around the tree first and backed it into the water. He flopped backward into it, splashed a big wake as the stern temporarily went under, then floated out into the river upright. I did the same thing and almost had it made but my kayak caught a cypress knee on one side and slowly began to turn broadside in the current. Moments later I was in the water. Again, it had only been a matter of seconds, but there was no stopping the capsize once the current began to turn my craft.

My Nikon D70, with which I had already shot about 500 photos that day, and the second camera I had gotten wet, was at my waist as I hit the water. When I was upright again, I dropped the camera in the seat of the kayak and went back ashore. I wiped myself down and slid back into the river again. This time the kayak floated into the river without incident and I was no worse for the wear other than being wet from baseball cap to the inside tip of my boots. Another camera was fried, however.

In midstream we noticed a water snake had chosen to cross the river in the shadow of the fallen oak. Chick moved back up to the north end and waited as the snake swam into the range of his camera. He continued to photograph as I sat in midstream, stewing because my camera had been reduced to the status of a big, wet, black paperweight. The battery shorted out the electronics, a knowledgeable friend told me. My favorite 28-200 zoom lens would dry out, I hoped, as it had the first time I took a dip in the river. The good news was that the compact flash card holding the digital photographs survived intact.

After Chick finished photographing the Banded Water Snake that seemed to have no problem going about its business swimming among the branches of the tree, we went under the Interstate-95 Bridge at fairly high speed for kayaks. We were hurrying for a reason. Earlier, Chick had told me the story of a man hit by bridge debris from a logging truck and killed while fishing on the river under an I-95 bridge in Georgia. Chick's friend, a doctor, had attended the victim who died on the way to the hospital. The repeat of such an event would have been a one in a trillion recurrence, but we didn't take any chances.

We crossed under the railroad trestle a mile and a quarter further, about 6.25 miles into the paddle, and I recalled the spot below the trestle where I had fished years ago with my brother-in-law Gilbert McRae. I had asked him then about the road noise.

Gilbert adjusted his fishing pole, pondered my question and finally said, "What noise?"

I suppose that's the best way to deal with the road rumble.

At Stafford's Bridge (U.S. Highway 301), 7.5 miles downriver, we met Larry Morris, a fisherman who lives between Lake View and Fairmont, N.C. Morris had failed to catch anything and was heading home. He didn't mind the road noise either, he said.

A cabin sits on a secluded section of the river between Harllees Bridge and Stafford's Bridge in Dillon County.

Dillon County Landing off Highway 57 east of Dillon has one of the most scenic settings on the river.

7

Riding The Flood To Dillon County Landing

Stafford's Bridge (U.S. 301) to Dillon County Landing (9 Miles)

It was mid-June and the swamp was still filled with water, so much of it that it flowed a foot deep across the dirt road leading from S.C. Highway 57 to Dillon County Landing, 9 miles downriver. The landing was our destination for the day and we came to park Chick's Subaru before loading his kayak in my truck for the drive back up to Stafford's Bridge. There was so much water at the landing that the river was almost 150 feet wide on the picturesque bend where a small picnic pavilion overlooks a stand of tall cypresses on the opposite bank. The river swept through the trees eight to ten feet up the trunks. The Little Pee Dee was at flood stage, over 9.5 feet at a measuring point on the intermediate destination at Highway 9, and the subject of a National Weather Service warning on local flooding. The river measurement scale only went to 10.4 feet and the crest of the flood was still to come.

The high water was mostly a good thing, we reasoned. We had encountered so many fallen trees in the upper section and had found the more water in the river, the easier it would be to go around the trees into the swamp and avoid portaging. At the same time, if we were stopped by a fallen tree, any portage would be a difficult one because the water would probably be between knee and waist deep in all the spots available. There would probably be no banks and no sandbars in sight anywhere this day

Earlier, when we completed the previous Harllees Bridge to Stafford's Bridge section, we had worried about an obstacle of brush and trees that spanned the river just below Stafford's. It looked then like we would be facing a portage before we ever left sight of the bridge. Now, barely two weeks later, the obstacle was gone, covered by the water surging down from Marlboro County.

Many miles above us, in that first section coming out of Red Bluff Lake, we knew the river would be roaring through the narrow turns. For a fleeting moment I wished we could be back up there to do it again. But we had met that challenge and, despite getting wet, had mastered it.

"I don't think we need helmets, but a life vest would help," Chick said as we unloaded the kayaks. He probably had in the back of his mind the fact that I had already capsized twice. Both times I had difficulty remounting the kayak in deep water after a portage but never felt in danger. Because of the flood warning we decided to start the trip wearing our bulky life jackets instead of the usual procedure of stowing them behind the seat with a fastener clipped to our belts.

On each of those two dunkings, I had fried the electronics in the camera I was carrying. And both times I had purchased another used digital single lens reflex online. The original had cost me over $1,000 new many years earlier. The second and the third, the one I now had in a watertight dry bag between my legs in the kayak, had each cost $110 used. I was willing to risk getting another camera wet to get quality shots.

We pushed off about 1130 on a Friday morning and calculated it would take five hours to cover the nine miles. Our first checkpoint for time and distance would be the S.C. Highway 9 Bridge, about 2.5 miles away. Thus far, we had taken about 20 percent longer in each section than expected. But this was the heaviest flow yet and if we could avoid multiple portages, we calculated we would reach Dillon County Landing ahead of schedule.

Halfway around the first bend, a newly fallen laurel oak spanned the river. Over a foot of rain had fallen in the past two weeks, including the torrential downpour from tropical storm Andrea, and the banks had been softened so much we expected to find many new fallen trees like the one ahead blocking our way. Chick spotted an opening at the midpoint of the fallen tree where the trunk was an inch or two under water. But leafy branches covered the possible opening. He rattled the limb with his paddle and, satisfied there was nothing live in the branches, adjusted his life vest and shoved the bow of his 10-foot Pungo into the opening. He slid in, grunted a couple of times, and disappeared into the wall of green.

Moments later he yelled, "I'm on the other side. Come on."

I followed him and slid through without incident also.

We had taken a bathroom break before getting in at Stafford's Bridge knowing there would be few places to stop along the way. Landowners routinely post "No Trespassing" signs on their property along the river and we were not going to take the chance of facing the business end of someone's 12-gauge while trying to explain a pee stop.

The Upper Little Pee Dee in flood moves quickly, probably more than 5 miles per hour. That does not sound fast, but combine the forward speed with narrow cuts where the flow is compressed and you find yourself on alert at all times. There was little possibility of making a course change once we started through an opening.

Mastering the first section from Red Bluff down to County Line Road had been something of a measuring stick and we both felt we had passed the test well enough to handle anything the Little Pee Dee could throw at us from here on down.

Despite the 27-mile Scenic River designation of the waterway in Dillon County and the remarkable natural beauty of the stretch, there is no escaping the road noise on the sections immediately around Dillon. We had first heard the faint rumble of Interstate 95 not long after leaving Harllees Bridge and it had become increasingly louder as we crossed under the interstate and headed for U.S. 301. Now we were leaving 301 and finally had behind us the sounds of the trucks and cars on I-95, and the local traffic on 301. U.S. 301 north from Dillon is also heavily traveled because it leads out to the I-95 exit that is flanked by South Of The Border, the well-known north-south stopping point graced by the massive roadside sombrero of Pedro, corporate symbol of the entertainment, lodging and dining center adjacent to the interstate.

The sounds of Highway 301 and I-95 began to fade and in its place came the less annoying rumble of traffic on the S.C. 9 Bridge between Dillon and Lake View. We passed a wide landing that apparently doubled as a swimming beach on a broad stretch of river at the 1.25 mile mark downstream. A wooden structure on the north end of the beach looked like a diving platform. And someone had set up a picnic table on the bank directly beside the river. The landing is at the end of Cypress Bluff Court, half a mile from a large Dillon suburb with dozens of homes. We crossed under the S.C. 9 Bridge and the abandoned road bridge just east of it after a little over two hours of paddling, 4.6 miles downriver. We had not yet been forced to portage but had twice made excursions into the swamp, wending our way through the swift flow around and among the big cypresses to bypass fallen oaks blocking the river.

A lone fisherman on the abandoned bridge had cast a spinning reel line with a pink and yellow bobber into the river.

"Had any luck?" I called up to the man.

"Haven't caught much of anything yet," he said. As noted earlier, the exchange was close to the closemouthed standard when meeting anglers on the river.

He wanted to know where we came from upriver and we told him.

"I don't know Red Bluff," he said.

Often, if you name a place just two or three stops upstream or downstream, the local person you are talking with will not know the destination. And when we talked about landings 10 miles or 50 or 100 away, the person we were talking with often reacted as if we were discussing a foreign land. Obviously, most of those who frequent the river confine themselves to a small local area.

Water coursed past the depth marker on the Highway 9 Bridge at 9.4 feet. The scale topped out at 10.1 feet. We wanted to make a bathroom stop and lunch break at the bridge but there was nothing but water everywhere. The put-in for boats was completely covered so we pushed on. Our lunches were in watertight compartments in the back of each kayak and we would need to wait for a real stopping point. Because it is difficult to turn safely in the seat of a kayak, when Chick needed something from his watertight storage I came alongside to get it out. And he did the same for me.

The single most beautiful part of this section in high water came 1.3 miles past the Highway 9 Bridge. The river on the north side opened into a large and relatively wide body of water covered with reeds and alligator weed. Narrow channels of black water striated the vegetation and led into the distance several hundred feet to the tree line. We ventured back along one of the open water trails and were rewarded with some of the most beautiful scenes on the river. We could not find bottom with our kayak paddles, which meant depths of more than six feet.

At another point, downriver from the first excursion, we entered a similar body of water on the south side of the river. We paddled in for a quarter mile or so before turning around. This time we missed the outlet and paddled in a circle for about ten minutes before letting the flow take us back to the river. We came out a quarter mile upstream from our entry. This knocked a significant hole in our theory that the bubbles on the water and the flow would always bring us back to the river downstream.

Dillon County Landing, just off River Access Dr. on S.C. 57 leading to Mullins, is a singularly beautiful location on the Little Pee Dee. The dirt road to the landing passes directly through the swamp and had been covered with a foot of water when we drove in that morning to leave Chick's car. Six hours later, there was even more water crossing the dirt road. At one point, a county deputy sheriff drove up to the far side of the water and then backed away, deciding discretion was the better choice for his low slung police cruiser.

When we pulled into the landing we were greeted by a crowd of people, most of them twentysomethings. They were letting off steam on a Friday afternoon and enjoying the cooling waters of the river at one of its most picturesque bends. One of the people I met said he was a frequent river visitor. Daniel Hayes of Dillon was planning a rubber tube float from the landing to the next bridge, Carmichael's, on the following weekend.

Hayes' friend, T.J. Boyd, said he was a logger and had been part of a crew cutting sections of the cypress forest upriver near Moccasin Bluff.

"You see any snakes there?" he asked.

"Just a couple of water snakes," I said.

"Well, when we cut timber at Moccasin Bluff we must have seen 75 moccasins in the swamp between us and the road," Boyd said. "Plenty of snakes."

Chick and I looked at each other and nodded, deciding not to openly challenge popular wisdom. We had heard so much about the water moccasins and other snakes but had seen few of them. We decided to reserve judgment until a very hot summer day on whether or not snakes were living in this section in overabundant numbers. To this point, we had seen no proof of that commonly-held belief.

Hayes, whose upper torso and arms were covered with tattoos, said he enjoyed his time on the river, particularly its serenity. Quiet was something he valued. He was like many of the young men and women you meet these days in the U.S., a war veteran with somber experiences hidden from the casual observer, usually brought out only if you ask in the right way.

He said he had done three combat tours in Afghanistan and one in Iraq during an eight year stint in the U.S. Army. He and I found an immediate common bond. We both had served at the same Army base in Germany, although my tour was a good bit earlier than his. Hayes said he was taking it easy these days. He had not yet made use of the GI Bill benefits he earned from his service and was just hanging out on this day with his loyal mutt, Chance, who jumped into the back of a pickup truck to pose with Daniel for a photograph.

"You have a good one," Hayes wished us.

"You too," I said.

One of the prime threats to the continued health and beauty of the Little Pee Dee was painfully obvious at Dillon County Landing. The place was littered with debris—broken bottles, the remains of campfires, plastic containers of every size and sort. It seemed nearly everyone who had visited had left a reminder of how little they cared for preserving one of the most beautiful spots on the river. I will be surprised if we find a more beautiful bend in the Little Pee Dee than this one, but it teeters on the verge of being an eyesore because of individual irresponsibility, government inability to enforce littering regulations and a general neglect for the welfare of the river. If every visitor picked up a single piece of trash, rather than just throwing something down, the place could be pristine again in a month.

The river opens on the north side 1.3 miles below Highway 9 bridge to reveal a wide body of water with multiple channels.

Daniel Hayes and his dog Chance take a break from swimming at Dillon County Landing.

Twin crosses above a deep cove on the river at Floydale Landing remember the lives of Jonathan and Martin.

8

Nije Važno And A Rumble On The River

Dillon County Landing to Carmichael's Bridge (8.5 Miles)

We came back to Dillon County Landing two weeks later at the end of June and before we could get the boats in the water a man in a Ford pickup stopped to issue a warning.

"In this high water, you're going to get lost in the swamp," he said after we told him our destination. The fellow riding with him nodded in agreement when he explained the problems on the multiple downstream channels through the swamp. We nodded and said thanks to the men in the pickup, both of us thinking but not verbalizing the fact that if we had come all the way down from Marlboro County, from places no one else seemed to go like Red Bluff, we ought to be able to work our way down a fairly wide 8.5-mile stretch between Dillon and Little Pee Dee State Park.

Conditions were good. The temperature was 80 going to 90. Possible thunderstorms were forecast later in the afternoon. Overhead, a few puffy clouds filtered the brilliant sunshine as we followed a trail of fast moving foamy, bubbles downriver. The water poured out of the swamp every few hundred yards, accelerating into cut-throughs that rerouted a part of the river at practically every bend. The flow was as quick as any day yet with the exception of the initial wild ride down from the headwaters at Red Bluff Lake five months earlier.

We pushed off at 11:15 with Chick leading. He paddled his dark green Wilderness 12-footer for a change. He had already strapped it on the car the previous night hoping his son Lin would join us. But Lin chose Columbia student nightlife over a day on the river and texted he wasn't going when he came in at 5 A.M.

For the first time, the paddling was easy from the beginning—few obstacles and plenty of straight sections. We passed the Little Pee Dee Shrine Club, which is between S.C.57 and the river, 1.8 miles down from Dillon County Landing. The Shrine Club sits beside the Schafer family compound, and is still a venue for dances and other events. The compound was home to Alan Schafer, a legendary businessman who grew a modest beer stand on the S.C.-N.C. state line along Highway 301 into a nationally-known entertainment and tourist attraction called South of the Border. When Interstate 95, complete with an interchange/exit-entrance, passed near the entertainment complex, South Of The Border became one of the favorite highway stops in the South. Schafer died in 2001 but the family business continues.

It seemed like no time before we heard the sounds of Floydale Bridge. In fact it was about two and a half hours, or 4.6 miles, much of it speedy paddling with no portages. We had been forced to turn into the swamp on a couple of occasions to get around fallen trees. But this was our fastest ride yet. We moved mostly in the shadows of the forest, emerging into direct sunlight only on wide bends. Otherwise, the canopy of the river swamp spared us from the direct heat of the sun and filtered its rays into long strands of light that arced through the branches and leaves and reflected on the water.

At Floydale Landing, after a lunch of chicken sandwiches and diet cola, Chick laid a towel on the gravel by the river bank and lay back with a bandana over his face. I found a seat out of the sun under a rickety steel shelter that had probably been nice before vandals broke most of the concrete chairs and all the tables.

We both were dozing in the shade when a sedan driven by a white-haired woman turned off the main highway, Lester Road. She was already committed to taking the circular drive that went past both of us and did so without making eye contact with me, only six feet away. I could see her staring at Chick's reclined form on the bank as she drove past. The license plate showed the car was from Fulton County, Ga. The woman stopped as far away from us as she could near the bridge. Three girls, most likely her grandchildren, bounded out of the car and started throwing rocks into the water in futile attempts to skip them across the river surface.

I wanted a picture of the bridge sign and kept my distance while walking past them with my camera held high to show my intentions. I waved the camera and said hello but the woman didn't acknowledge me. She turned her back to the children and acted as a one-person cordon between me and the girls as I went by a good 20 feet from them. I continued walking to the bridge, about 150-feet away, and carried out my customary assignment of photographing the bridge sign for any information it provided. As I was taking pictures I heard car tires scorching pavement and looked back to see the sedan bounce onto the road with the rear wheels throwing up a shower of gravel. Chick was standing where the car had been parked, hands on hips and a confused look on his face.

"I was just trying to show the girls how to skip a rock," he said. "I told them they ought to come up to Rabun County in North Georgia where there were lots of good flat rocks to throw. The lady piled them all in the car and they drove off just like that."

After the many friendly encounters along the river this was the first carload we had sent packing. The woman had not seen our kayaks in the tall grass about fifteen feet below the landing and must have assumed we wandered out of the swamp on foot. Our possessions seemed limited to my camera and the beat-up old backpack that Chick had been using for a pillow. Perhaps the biker's bandana atop his head, the too-short shirt he wore open at the top and bottom and the ragged NBA-length gym shorts hanging low at his hips had pushed the lady's protection meter into the red zone. Anyway, they missed out on what would have been a good talk with Chick during which they would have learned something about the river, rock skipping, our family and most probably quite a few more serendipitous facts on life in general.

Nije važno, not important, I thought of the moment and what my Bosnian friends often say about anything beyond individual control.

We were left with ourselves and the realization that there were two white-painted wooden crosses nailed to trees in front of us near the bridge. The transverse of each cross had the date *6 22 03* written in script. One was inscribed with 'Jonathan' and the second with 'Martin'. The two had apparently drowned near the spot. Perhaps the lady who fled with her grandchildren thought something even more untoward had occurred on the spot and that we had come back to reprise the deed.

Helen Belden Moody, whose website, http://www.helenslittlecorner.net/ has a variety of historical archives, later researched the markers and found a Dillon

Herald newspaper story which identified the two drowning victims as Jonathan Lee Matthews, 6, of Dillon and Efren Aguilar Estevez, 20, of Fairmont, N.C.

While I was photographing the crosses and Chick was skipping stones in the river the fellow who had worried about us getting lost in the swamp pulled up at the landing in his pickup. He seemed surprised to see us.

"I see you made it," he said with what seemed the slightest tinge of disappointment in his voice.

"We didn't have any problems," I responded cheerfully. "Do you know the river from here down?"

He shook his head. "No, we're up from around Lumberton," he said. "We're just out killing time." He drove off without offering further advice and we packed the kayaks.

Before we got under way Chick photographed the white sand ridge behind the landing. As he did, a man riding a small farm tractor emerged from the swamp pulling a trailer. He drove along the trail atop the ridge, crossed the highway and descended a dirt road which led to a house and outbuildings on the downstream side of the bridge.

Wayne Small lives in a home on the river near the Floydale Bridge landing.

When we got to the landing in front of the house I stopped and called to the man. He came out to the dock. He was Wayne Small and had lived there in the cove below the bridge for the past 12 years. He had done a great deal of work to try and stop the almost inevitable erosion of the river into his land, he said. Great quantities of bricks, other masonry and rocks had been poured into the curve where the river constantly ate into the bank.

"My family is coming from Georgia and I'm getting ready for the visit," he said. "We've had high water and I'm trying to fix it so they can drive into the place."

Chick was waiting in the next bend in the shadows under an oak that many years ago stopped its vertical growth and now grew parallel to the water, stretching at least 50 feet unsupported over the river.

"I guess we scared those people off," Chick said, still pondering why anyone would pass up a chance at conversation. I told him he was wearing the answer to his question. His river outfit shouted Salvation Army reject, I said. He returned the favor by reminding me that I had on a faded, torn long sleeve shirt that had seen better times in a previous decade, that my face was streaked white in a couple of places by sunscreen carelessly applied, that I wore a white embroidered cloth table napkin on the top of my head so that it fell down over the back of my neck French Foreign Legion style. And that my steel-rimmed glasses glinted sinisterly from under the bill of the $2 dirt-stained orange baseball cap I had recently purchased at Habitat for Humanity. Touché.

We considered improving our appearance in case of further encounters downriver, but after a couple of seconds deliberation agreed people would have to take us as we were. After all, we accepted everyone we met in the same spirit. Afterwards, the three miles plus down to Little Pee Dee State Park Landing were little more than a quick paddle. The river stayed wide and although we had to cross under two fallen oaks spanning the river, we moved briskly.

The regular landing at the State Park was still under high water but we paddled up the roadway for a short distance hoping to find a spot to get out. There was none. The truck was parked alongside the first of the two bridges only a quarter of a mile away. The river forks around an island and the second bridge, the one on the south side, is actually Carmichaels Bridge. So we came back to the main channel and stayed in the right fork, finally stopping in the swamp just above the bridge. It was a poor takeout, mostly covered in underbrush with a menacing broken limb weighing at least a couple of hundred pounds hanging directly above where we came ashore. We pushed into the bushes single file and moved as quickly as possible out of the shadow of the limb.

A man stopped to take pictures of the river while we were putting the kayaks in the truck. He said he was from Pennsylvania and wanted to know if the water was always so black. I told him about the tannin coloration and Chick explained that as soon as the level dropped it would begin to take on an orange-gold coloring from the white sand bottom. The man, clad in long gym shorts and a sleeveless t-shirt, said he had come down from Pennsylvania for a job interview at Harbor Freight, a big tool distribution center between Latta and Dillon. He didn't know if he had gotten the job as maintenance supervisor. We wished him luck, loaded the kayaks in the truck and drove back up to Dillon County Landing.

At the landing we found an even rowdier version of the lively crowd we had encountered two weeks earlier. People stood in clusters around four cars parked at different spots on the landing. Young people, probably teens, crowded around one car. Older twenty and thirty-something men roughhoused and talked loudly beside another car. Beer seemed to be doing a good job of lubricating that group. More young people gathered under the beat-up grill shelter by the river near the other two cars. Suddenly a muscular man with shaved head, a load of body tattoos and wearing only cargo shorts and sandals, chased a tall, slender man across the grass. I thought they were playing, much as the friendly fellows had done two weeks earlier at the same spot, until I heard the dull thud of a fist slam into the back of the younger man, knocking him down in the grass. The one I now identified as Mr.

Tattoo flattened the younger man and kicked him on the ground. He punched at the downed man's head.

The man on the ground pulled himself into a fetal position as the blows rained down. People from the group under the shelter screamed for the man to stop his assault. A woman with a few tattoos of her own crossed the sand, took Mr. Tattoo's arm and led him back to his group by the car. One of the men shoved a beer can into his hand. The beaten man crawled to his feet and headed for the shelter. He and his companions piled into a battered sedan and drove away from the landing at speed; the beaten man screamed unintelligibly from the back of the departing car until it was out of sight on the dirt road leading to Highway 57. If that fellow owned a gun, it sounded like he was going to get it, I told Chick. We'd probably read about the end of this fight in the newspaper in a week or so. One of them would be dead and the other in jail.

A beaver lodge and the telltale holes made by a pileated woodpecker on a dead tree share space along the bank near Carmichael's Bridge.

The river is a sanctuary for most people who use it. The man who chose to stage an assault there might just as well have done it in a church. He didn't deserve to be there if he couldn't appreciate the beauty of the river. Those who fight, get drunk or doped out there, or spread their litter on the landing, should all be banned.

Two more cars drove away, leaving a few children with some young adults swimming in the river. We rushed to get the kayaks tied down before an impending thunderstorm hit with full force. We pulled away from the landing with the swimmers still in the water. The sky in the direction of Dillon was black at 5 P.M. and Chick texted me minutes later that he hit a tropical downpour with severe lightning in town.

On the ride back to Fork Retch, after a day on the river, I normally replay the events of our paddle. Who we met, what we saw. The journey writes itself long before I get it all on paper. The rumble of my old truck and the whine of the knobby off-road tires normally contribute to a happy sort of river afterglow. But this day there was no such emotion. I could still hear the thump of fists and feet on a human body, violent thuds that sounded much like the dull, almost empty noise of a palm slapping a ripe watermelon.

Our days on the river are almost uniformly peaceful. We paddle, we observe, we sometimes go for miles without speaking, just photographing. It is a sheltered existence that shuts out nearly everything but the passage of nature in its remarkable complexity. On this day one man beating another robbed us of that peace, at least momentarily, and served as a reminder that although the river is beautiful, it is only a temporary escape. The rest of the world is out there and we must deal with that fact each time we come off the water.

A Red-Bellied Watersnake takes the sun seemingly oblivious to nearby paddlers. Photo L.L. Gaddy

9

Fallen Trees Everywhere

Carmichael's Bridge to Allen's Bridge (12 Miles)

We set out on a Sunday morning in late July from the landing at Pee Dee State Park upriver from Carmichael's Bridge. Our destination was Allen's Bridge, 12 miles downriver, just west of the Dillon County-Marion County boundary line. The Heritage Trust landing where we put in is located on the north side of the river, upstream from Carmichael's alongside a classic 30-acre Carolina bay. The South Carolina Department of Natural Resources explains that "Carolina Bays are elliptical or oval depressions of uncertain origin found in North and South Carolina, along with a few bays in Georgia, Virginia and Delaware. They are considered to be a freshwater wetland, most often isolated. The bay's depression fills with rainwater, usually in winter and spring, and dries in the summer months. This water level determines the plants and animals that inhabit the bay."[12]

The weather was hot and steamy as we pushed off at 11. Late afternoon thunderstorms were forecast, as they are practically every day during this part of the year. Our halfway point would be Huggins Bridge, where S.C. Highway 41 crosses the river, two miles north of the crossroads town of Fork between Marion and Lake View. The straight line distance between the two bridges was about three miles and the river trip was 5.8, possibly six miles, with a few detours away from the river and the long way around on oxbows. It would be another 6.6 miles from there down to Allen's Bridge.

At the first bend in the river we came upon a familiar problem that would repeat itself often for the next eight hours. A massive laurel oak, with its full foliage intact, had fallen across the river, blocking it completely. Recent heavy rains and the resulting high water had washed out the roots and toppled the tree. A trail of bubbles from the swift water crossing an upstream obstruction diverted into the swamp behind the massive, pancake-shaped root ball of the oak. By now we knew the routine: Chick followed the bubbles and I followed Chick. We floated behind the tree and into its dark shadow, then crossed the swamp floor atop a few inches of rapidly moving water, bumping and banging through the cypress knees. Three minutes later we exited the swamp into the river a hundred feet downstream.

Every few bends we came upon another fallen tree. Each one proved a unique problem requiring its own solution. On the upper river, where the downed trees were smaller, there had often been a portion of the tree that was submerged. There we aimed for the opening at speed and bumped over the top of the trunk or a large limb. But there was no bumping or log jumping from Carmichael's to Allen's Bridge. The trees were too large.

Occasionally, where the river was more than 100-feet wide, we would find a way though the uppermost branches of the tree at the end where it touched the bank. If we could see the water flowing on the other side of the branches, there was a good chance we could make it through: Get up speed, duck your head and let the kayak push through.

Only the initial stretch from the headwaters at Red Bluff Lake proved more challenging in the first hour. Carmichael's to Allen's Bridge is considerably wider on average than the Red Bluff run, but surprisingly, in the tight sections it is even narrower than upriver, sometimes only 25 feet across, and the flow seemed just as quick despite the lower water. As on the upper river there were places where alternating fallen trees from both sides still allowed passage but demanded precise turning. In the first hour we sweated heavily and pulled hard on the paddles to make the required left-right turns and work our way through.

The second hour began just as the first with another downed tree. The river had cut a two-foot-wide opening along the bank just beyond the top of the tree in the river and we scooted through. Shortly afterward we encountered a small settlement of what appeared to be at least five homes on the north bank of the river. The houses, all modern structures, are at the end of the dirt road to the right off State Park Road. That road is opposite the dirt track that leads to the landing above Carmichael's Bridge where we put in. This would be a good point to take out if problems occurred or to put in if one of the locals allowed it. One of the houses had a good sand boat ramp protected by bulkheads. However, there are so many "No Trespassing" signs on the river you have to be especially careful of private property rights.

About 90 minutes into the paddle we tried a cut-through and got halfway across the swamp with the downriver bend in sight through the trees. At that point another fallen tree blocked our water detour and there was no choice but to drag our kayaks across the swamp floor bumping through the cypress knees until we pushed our craft back into the river beyond yet another fallen oak.

Area resident William Rouse tries his luck with a spinning reel above Huggins Bridge Landing.

At 2 p.m., after three hours on the water, we met two boats coming upstream. A family of four was fishing from their electric-powered Creek Boat. They were preceded by a fiberglass one-man electric boat piloted by area resident William Rouse, who was wielding a casting reel. I had met Rouse earlier that morning at the Pee Dee State Park landing after I checked the depth of the big mud puddles in my truck on the road going in to the landing. He said then he had decided to drive down to Huggins Landing in his four-wheel-drive pickup and put in there.

On the next turn we confronted another fallen oak. There was a narrow opening at what had been the top of the tree and the two boats, each larger than our kayaks, had made it through so we entered the opening without pause. The boaters we passed would not be able to go much further, however, because another quarter mile upstream from where we met them, as already noted, we had been forced to get out and walk through the swamp.

We moved on downstream without further obstacles and arrived at Huggins Bridge at 2:30. We found Rouse's pickup backed up to the water and felt like he wouldn't mind us using his tailgate for a picnic lunch seat. Chick had his favorite summertime river meal of spiced, boiled shrimp and boiled peanuts washed down with lemonade. I stuck with a bland turkey sandwich and diet cola.

Huggins Landing was a bit cleaner than most of the places we had stopped coming down the river, but calling it a landing is a stretch. It is really an opening beside the river bridge without a paved boat ramp, just a sandy bank where trailers can be backed down near the water. A sign on a tree advertised boat motor repairs. A graffiti-smeared picnic shelter near the water offered protection from the sun or rain but little more. There was no place to sit. While we were there a couple of cars pulled through the parking lot blaring music. The youngish occupants eyed us as if we were aliens and we returned the favor from under our cap bills trying to smile all the while.

When we pushed off at 3:05 we both assumed the worst was over, that we would reach Allen's Bridge in a little over two hours.

Bad assumption.

Just because the river was relatively wide at Huggins Bridge had no effect on the frequency of obstacles. The fallen oak at the end of the first straightaway was the most massive we had yet seen on the river. It was at least 100 feet long and the trunk so large and the foliage so dense, it blotted out a clear view of the water downstream.

The tree had been down for only a short while but the river had already created a narrow channel on the backside in the shadow of the massive pancake-shaped root mound. Chick moved into the opening, twisted and turned in his kayak and after a couple of minutes found a way through. I tried to do the same, but could not get my longer kayak to turn, hanging up each time on a cypress knee growing at just the wrong spot.

Finally, within touching distance of the root mound, which towered a good 15 feet above me, I got out and wrestled with my kayak to get it turned toward the river. My boots sank in the mud and made a sucking sound each time I pulled one out and stepped forward. Finally I got the craft at the angle I needed to get back in the river, straddled the cockpit and dropped backward into the seat. From there I pushed my hands down into the mud on one side and then the other, monkey-walking until I was back in the river where the fast current immediately caught the

The route from Carmichael's Bridge to Allen's Bridge is marked by the large number of fallen trees spanning the river.

bow and pulled me downstream. On this day neither of us capsized despite the swift water and the frequent, often awkward mounting and dismounting. My last dunking had been at the I-95 Bridge at Dillon. Our score on capsizes stood at two for me and one for Chick and we were doing our best to hold it there.

A Red-bellied Watersnake, *Nerodia erythrogaster*, seemed unafraid of us as it sunned atop the trunk of a fallen tree in the river. Both of us snapped pictures at will from five or six feet away for a couple of minutes before the snake slid into the water, swam to the base of the submerged tree and emerged again on an exposed root. For the first time we consistently heard and occasionally saw snakes along the river dropping off low limbs and downed trunks. The splash, more like a kerplunk, usually came about 50 feet ahead. But occasionally the snakes would drop off just as we passed, often within a paddle length of the boat. They preferred spots within foliage and the branches of downed trees where sunlight penetrated but did not reveal them.

Most of the turtles sunning on logs dropped off before we were 200 feet or more away. But just above Huggins Bridge a soft-shelled turtle stayed in position until I was within two paddle lengths away. Chick speculated that the noise of the cars on the bridge may have distracted the turtle. Twice we rounded a curve and large deer were drinking from the river. In both cases, by the time we had our cameras up the only sign of the deer was the sound of splashing water in the swamp as they ran away.

This section was added proof that a 10-foot kayak is the better choice for the upper reaches of the Little Pee Dee. Time and again, Chick was able to move in and out of tight situations where the additional two feet of my kayak hung me up on cypress knees or limbs, sometime leading to dangerous situations in deep water. And in the swamp, where we had already spent considerable time since entering the river at Red Bluff Lake, he made the narrow turns with ease while I bumped along, often being forced to get out and walk. By the end of the day we had dealt with at least two dozen trees that blocked the channel. But in a couple of weeks, I knew, the advantages of my longer craft would finally emerge. The trips through the swamp would end until high water returned in the fall and once we hit the wide water below Fork Retch, the 12-footer would glide more easily, requiring less paddling effort.

It was a quarter until seven when we crossed between the pilings holding up the concrete slabs on Allen's Bridge. There was no boat landing and we stepped out into two feet of water while straddling our kayaks. In that depth of water, it takes a sort of bowlegged waggle walk to avoid falling over while working your way to shore with the kayak between your legs. As we hauled our craft up the steep, sandy bank, we did what we could to avoid a fierce swarm of mosquitoes intent on dining at sunset.

Carmichael's Bridge to Allen's Bridge is not for the casual paddler. There's too much to do, battling downed trees, river obstacles and poison ivy and avoiding the increased number of snakes. At low water a boater handy with a chain saw might be able to open up the waterway a bit and do everyone a great favor. But the fallen trees are so large it would be a monumental task to free up a real channel on this section of the river. I don't expect any Good Samaritan to do that in the near future.

Take to this section forewarned. It is a long slog. But a good one.

A three-quarter-mile long straight stretch precedes the railroad trestle between Nichols and Mullins six miles downriver from Allen's Bridge.

10

Return To Mosquito Beach

Allen's Bridge to Fork Retch (9)

Allen's Bridge crosses the Little Pee Dee one mile north of the Marion County Line on Buck Swamp Road, a heavily rutted dirt two lane that connects Fork in Dillon County with Nichols in Marion County via paved highway on each end. It was there that I met Chick and his son Lin on the last Saturday morning in August for the paddle to my house on Fork Retch, nine miles downriver.

The first four miles to Old Nichols Highway Bridge were an unknown. Would they be as challenging as the previous run from Carmichaels Bridge? Or just an easy paddle like the second section of the day, from Old Nichols Bridge to The Retch? There was one certainty about the day's schedule: We would stop at Mosquito Beach on our Uncle C.P. Mincey's farm. The beach, a dreary-looking little piece of swamp below the railroad trestle, had been the starting point for our first outdoor adventures half a century earlier when Chick's dad had built a fishing cabin there. Eventually the Mincey, Gaddy and Walker families showed up there to camp, to wet a hook and be together.

Lin, starting his senior year at Carolina, would be along for the paddle to listen to tales of our youthful exploits on the river, most of them circa Dwight Eisenhower's presidency, a time when his grandfather Big Chick Gaddy was master of the Little Pee Dee's best fishing spots. The route down from Allen's Bridge began with a long, pleasant one mile goodbye to Dillon County. We had been in the county for ten separate trips including the 27-mile scenic river water trail from Moccasin Bluff Landing to Huggins Bridge on Highway 41 outside Fork. The journey had taken us from the isolation of Marlboro County to the path around Dillon, including the tumult of traffic associated with Interstate 95 and U.S. highway 301 and finally back into the quiet below Dillon County Landing. Now we would pass out of the county and enter Marion for a six-mile stretch. After that, at Fork Retch, we would begin a 58-mile journey that would almost always have Horry County on our left and Marion on our right. Now and then the river strays completely into one county of the other.

A few minutes downriver our paddling came to a stop.

"There, look, on the riverbank," Chick said. I thought he finally had the classic shot of a water moccasin he had sought since the launch from the headwaters at Red Bluff in February.

"It's a cardinal," he said.

I looked for a bird.

"A cardinal flower," he said. "It blooms in September."

There on the riverbank, *Lobelia cardinalis*, the cardinal flower, a brilliant red perennial, had caught Chick's eye from 100 feet away. It's found in wet areas, he told us, and pollinated by hummingbirds. I eased my kayak into shore and photographed the blooming flower from a few feet away until Chick, in his excitement at the sighting, edged in with his kayak and eased me out of the way to get up close. It did, indeed, have the color of a cardinal's robe. In research later I found the plant had all kinds of medicinal uses, none more interesting than as a love potion. But the mixture can be toxic if consumed in large quantities, the source of my research cautioned.[13]

The pattern for the day developed soon after our stop for the cardinal. Lin had no patience with our deliberate pace and paddled ahead, then doubled back upriver to join us. We had our routine developed after months on the river photographing plant and animal life, looking for exceptionally large or old trees and generally enjoying the river experience. Lin was youth and youth wants to go faster, to outstrip the old. So he started circling us and kept it up all day. His going

The brilliant cardinal flower, a favorite of hummingbirds, grows along the river.

ahead worked for him but limited our photography of snakes, turtles and birds. Most of them flee at the first sign of a kayak and on this section we saw hardly a wild animal, save a lone turtle and the flashes of white tails as deer bounded from the water's edge into the swamp.

But having him along with a different set of eyes, different thinking on what the river experience means, outweighed the short-term drawbacks. As a toddler he had been taught by Chick to respect all creatures, to include the tiniest insects, and he never killed anything, not mosquitoes or bugs or snakes. As a young man he already held a genuine respect for nature and preserving the environment.

Early on each of us had our little adventure for the day. Chick came within inches of hitting a large wasp nest as he took a shortcut under a branch. Lin got hung up on a log after trying one of our Little Pee Dee jumps. He managed to hop himself off. And I floated into the branches of an overhanging oak as I let my kayak drift backwards, photographing Chick and Lin paddling under an archway of limbs. Luckily no harm done to any of us—no snakes in the kayak, no angry wasps, no capsizing.

Will and Clarice Walker ran a small corner grocery in Nichols not far from the Lumber River Bridge.

The real value of the day was immediately clear to me, watching Chick and Lin talk their way down the river, obviously comfortable in each other's company. I recalled my boyhood years with my father. He worked nearly every day at the corner grocery he ran and I can think of perhaps only a dozen times, at most, that we spent alone doing some fun activity. In his 72nd and last year we were alone often, but that was quite different. He was terminally ill. The fathers of the Baby Boom generation, the men who came back from World War II, were fulltime breadwinners and by and large had little time to spare for their children. They were too busy trying to carve out a new life and provide for their families.

One of my best memories of my father, who was the finest man I have known, was a full day on the Lumber and the Little Pee Dee, just the two of us. Even though that was nearly sixty years ago, it remains one of the nicest days of my life and a reminder to parents that time spent with their kids is crucial to shaping a happy childhood. My dad also took me for a flight on my sixth birthday. And he gave me a Brownie camera when I was not much older. In retrospect, I can see that in the limited time we had together, he had introduced me to the river, to photography and to aviation, all pursuits I have followed my entire life. My mother Clarice Blanton Walker had been an excellent writer who passed along her love of the written word and literature to me. She encouraged me often to be on the river and to write about my experiences.

We came alongside a well-maintained house and outbuildings on the south bank about three-quarters of a mile inside the Marion County line. The house was part of a compound at the end of the only named road leading into this section, on Black Water Court off Jackson Farm Court. Soon after Chick and Lin debated the best way to go under an oak blocking the river. Chick told him to lean back and tilt his eyes to the sky to go under. Lin disagreed. Leaning forward is the best way to do it, he said. In the end Chick leaned back and Lin leaned forward. Both methods worked.

"Whatever you tell him, he does the opposite," Chick said afterwards, perhaps unaware that his voice carried a tone of approval, an acknowledgment that his son could make his own decisions and learn from his mistakes when the wrong choice was made.

We encountered two more cabins another mile and a half downriver. The first was a simple river dwelling on concrete pilings. A barbecue grill and plastic chairs flanked the front door and a picture window. Stairs led off each end of the porch which had no railings. Grass grew a foot high in the little yard fronting the river. The place was simple, adequate, in keeping with the isolated section of river and cypress swamp beyond. The next turn was blocked by a downed oak and we were forced to backtrack and paddle into the swamp, where the shallow water swirled and bubbled across a surprisingly clean-looking white sand bottom that shone gold-colored in the brief flashes of sunlight. Chick and I moved between the big cypress trees at double speed, bumping along against the submerged knees before emerging downriver ahead of Lin. Chick had advised him to follow us but he had chosen to go the other away, through the swamp behind the root ball of the fallen tree. His way worked also.

At this point, in brilliant sunshine, I had a visitor. A dragonfly landed on the prow of my kayak. I zoomed in on it with the full extension of my 55-300 millimeter lens and marveled at the shape of the insect hitching a ride.

"Did you ever notice a dragonfly looks a lot like a Huey helicopter?" I called out.

"Maybe," Chick said.

A dragonfly hitches a ride downriver toward Mosquito Beach.

I watched this curious creature magnified to King Kong proportions in my viewfinder as the kayak drifted on its own. The dragonfly's eyes are marvels of nature, capable of providing a 360 degree range of vision. The large, transparent wings and long stabilizer tail enable it to fly up, down, left, right, forward and backward. Further examination of the wings revealed two sets, one longer than the other, like some biplanes.

This winged passenger two feet from me was a classic predator whose penchant for dining on mosquitos made it a good friend, one welcome to the free ride. If I pressed Chick he could probably have laid out the classification for me. I didn't say anything, just watched quietly through the camera viewfinder. Later I did some research. Dragonfly—Kingdom—*Animalia*, Phylum—*Arthropoda*, Class—*Insecta*, Order—*Odonata* and Suborder—*Anisoptera*. Unlike my talented cousin, who has this sort of information permanently stored in his capacious brain, moments after I move on from writing this I will have forgotten most of the classification. But I will remember those 360-degree eyes and the ability to fly in all six directions the next time I take off in my Cessna where it is a victory to simply aviate straight and level. After a couple of minutes, I heard Chick warn Lin about overhanging poison ivy dead ahead. I put down my camera, lifted my paddle to avoid the vegetation and watched my visitor lift off the prow, presumably headed out on a mosquito search and destroy mission.

We crossed under a large overhead power line about 4 miles downriver and a few moments later heard a vehicle rumbling onto the Old Nichols Highway Bridge. The sound only mildly disturbed the silence of the river and just two more vehicles passed in the time it took us to approach, float under and depart the bridge area. Despite appearing to be in the middle of nowhere the landing at the bridge is only a ten-minute walk to a good country store at the intersection of Gilchrist Road and Old Nichols Highway on the ridge above the river.[14] Lana Allread took over the place from her father Walter years ago and is the niece of my high school football teammate Ernest Allread. Both Ernest and Walter passed away during the years I was overseas.

From the bridge the river wanders left and right in six, short, uncomplicated bends before a three-quarter mile long straight leading to the railroad trestle between Nichols and Mullins. These days the Little Pee Dee trestle and another one on the Lumber River side of Nichols have been rated unsafe for heavy loads by inspectors and the railroad company says it doesn't have the money to make repairs. So the big trains don't run anymore.

Shortly after leaving the Old Nichols Highway Bridge you pass Huggins Landing, the back side of a farm owned by Norman Huggins. His father, Lawton, was the Marion County game warden for many years, and Norman is a retired Air Force colonel whose F-101 supersonic Voodoo fighter was hit by antiaircraft fire over North Vietnam in 1965. He ejected off the coast east of Hai Phong and was rescued before capture. Norman had flown 140 combat missions out of Thailand and Vietnam at the time of his shootdown and soon afterwards was returned to the

Retired Air Force fighter pilot Col. Norman Huggins above a diving platform on the deep bend at Huggins Landing farm.

U.S. The town of Mullins staged a victory parade for him and gave him the key to the city when he got home. He lives most of the year in Valdosta, Ga., but returns to the family home on the river many times each year. "My great great grandfather Solomon bought the farm, which originally extended upriver beyond the railroad trestle," Huggins said. "The upper part of the farm was taken by eminent domain for the railroad right of way," he said. "If they ever stop using the railroad, I'm going to try and get that land back."

We passed a diving platform just above Huggins Landing at one of the deepest coves on the Little Pee Dee. In high water the depth may reach 20 feet, Norman Huggins told me one day when I visited the farm with him. Just beyond the diving platform is a sunken area in the bank where local legend says two Confederate deserters hid at the end of the war. "I have been told that the local people ran them out when the war ended," he said. "Anyway, from the look of the bank, there could have been a cave down there."[15]

We floated the straight stretch leading up to the railroad trestle with only infrequent paddle strokes to maintain direction. At 2:30 p.m., three hours after launch, I went under the trestle first and turned to photograph Chick and Lin passing below the silver span. We were nearly six miles downriver.

Another of my high school teammates, Johnny Lane, has a home just below the trestle and each year pulls out some of the largest Red Breasts caught along this stretch of the river. Just after passing under the trestle near Johnny's house, we finally saw an alligator, the first one on the river. But it was a green and yellow plastic toy blowup model hanging deflated in the branches of a tree along the river bank. Moments after the faux alligator sighting we arrived at Mosquito Beach. We stopped to pay our respects to the shell of the cabin where Big Chick Gaddy cooked some of his finest fish stews, told tall tales and consumed considerably more than the daily per capita average of whiskey. The cabin was the creation of

Big Chick and Timmonsville carpenter Toy Skinner. The precise location is a spot on the water just below Redbreast Ridge along the river side of C.P.'s land.

Mosquito Beach, named for the insect that afflicts anyone who enters into this swamp, consists of about five feet of off-white sand which appears near the front door at extreme low water. Red Breast Ridge, the land above the river where C.P. once kept his hogs, was named by his son Charles. The cabin, 5.85 miles downriver from Allen's Bridge, was constructed from loads of salvaged lumber hauled in by Big Chick and assembled with the assistance of Skinner. The architectural design was by committee and apparently whoever held a hammer had design authority for the day.

Father and son Chick and Lin Gaddy visit the old cabin at Mosquito Beach.

The place was built directly on the river just above the deep cut of a bend, which means that in high water the river sweeps under and sometimes through the cabin. There were some bunks in a large open room with a cook stove on one side where Big Chick worked his magic. The back porch was built directly over muddy swamp bottom. On the front side, a roof extension covered steps that ended only a couple of feet from the water. Ten feet to the left an artesian well once spilled clean water out of a pipe drilled in the dark, swamp bottom. It no longer flows. The one luxury inside the cabin had been an indoor bathroom plumbed to a buried 55-gallon drum which served as a septic tank.

"Furnishing the club house was easy since Uncle Chick had access to surplus army materials," Charles Mincey recalled. "That included surplus Army bunk beds, etc. The front door was famous, at least to us, since it had a connection to one of the Pee Dee area's most famous sons, Melvin Purvis, the FBI agent who shot the gangster John Dillinger. The door came off Melvin's father's house. An old army locker was always stocked with emergency food – Army K Rations. The K Rations contained a few special treats, cigarettes and chocolate candy. Cousin Bill's father, Uncle Will, and Uncle Chick kept their Pepsi (code word for Beer) in an old refrigerator. An AM radio provided nighttime entertainment."

Betty Mincey recalled all the nights she spent in the cabin with C.P. "He loved to go down there," she said. "We would all be there on Saturday night, me and the children, Cindy and Charles and Kenneth. And the trains would be crossing the trestle like they were coming inside the cabin. He would play the radio and he loved it. We didn't." My uncle's favorite song on those mosquito-plagued hot summer nights on the river was the George Jones rendition of Little Milton's "Grits Ain't Groceries." Little Milton and songwriter Titus Turner obviously knew a thing or two about love with lyrics which began,

"If I don't love you, baby
Grits ain't grocery
Eggs ain't poultry
And Mona Lisa was a man©[16]

C.P. Mincey at the helm of the family boat on the Little Pee Dee.

Big Chick and C.P.'s cabin no longer exhibits even a shadow of its former glory. The roof is green with mold like a Swiss mountain house with a grass-covered roof. The steps and floor have rotted and most of the windows are broken. The building barely stands upright on stacks of rickety cement blocks no longer precisely aligned one atop the other. The place could topple over at any moment. I expect it, or big parts of it, to someday come floating down The Retch, or at the least to hang up at the S.C. Highway 76 Bridge above The Retch.

There is a walkway down from the Mincey house on Gilchrist Road to the river. Today it goes past a newer cabin built on a fishing lake C.P. created by diverting water from the local creek. The new body of water was christened Swine Lake honoring the hog trade that helped my uncle finance some of the construction and excavation. His son Charles also gets credit for naming the second cabin and lake.

The star of Mosquito Beach was Lacy Lamar Big Chick Gaddy, a larger than life family legend. He was the husband of my mother's sister Bessie Evelyn, who was always Aunt Sally to us. She had once also been called Big Sally because of her long legs and skill at basketball as a teenager. Big Chick was a heavy-set man, well under six feet, with a large head and thinning, greased down, long strands of black hair pulled straight back over a white scalp. His face was dominated by a large nose and cheeks pocked from childhood acne. When he spoke, his Southern drawl was loud and crackly. And in between he made growling sounds and often grunted with the skill of a grizzled, old Army sergeant, which he was.

Despite his gravelly voice he was a friendly, good-humored man who enjoyed people, life on the river and cooking fish stew. And he was always friendliest toward late afternoon, when he sipped his favorite beverage, William Penn whiskey. In his honor on the farm there is a spot Charles dubbed William Penn Place. It celebrates the restorative powers of the libation Big Chick called his leg medicine.

Big Chick reveled in telling stories, most often fishing tales or accounts of his service overseas in World War II. His tales were happy ones and he accompanied them with infectious laughter that rumbled up from his ample belly. Most of my youth he ran the National Guard armory in Timmonsville. Big Chick and Big Sally had three sons. Stan is the youngest preceded by Ed and the oldest, Lacy Lamar Gaddy, Jr., my paddling companion. Like the rest of us, he enjoyed listening to Big Chick's stories and recalled with an inheritance of his father's good humor that "Dad won the war as a supply sergeant at Greenham Common, England. Just him and Ike."

Lacy Lamar Big Chick Gaddy was the architect and chief cook of the cabin at Mosquito Beach.

As a boy I was convinced Big Chick and Ike had indeed run the whole WWII European operation. Years later when I visited Greenham Common I found Ike reminders everywhere but none dedicated to Big Chick. Obviously an oversight easily corrected if we could get Charles to visit and call upon his naming muse.

Big Chick discovered the medicinal value of whiskey early on in life and never strayed from the certainty that it bolstered his health, primarily helping his bad leg. Some days he would tap his right knee to denote where the liquid relief flowed and then the next week would shift over to his left leg. He always kept a bottle or two of William Penn under the sink at his house in Timmonsville and more bottles at the cabin on Mosquito Beach. He drank it, he cooked with it and probably rubbed it on both legs.

Big Chick Gaddy enjoyed fishing and preparing his special fish stew recipe.

Big Chick was one of the best anglers on the river and routinely brought a stringer full of fish home from any trip. He prepared his stew at Mosquito Beach with the bottle of William Penn in its customary place beside the cook stove. The recipe was as secret as the planning of the D-Day Landings. But we knew the ingredients involved periodic additions of two shots of William Penn in the stew and one for the cook. Some nights he reversed the formula, ingesting two medicinal doses, perhaps one for each leg, before pouring one in the stew. We called it catfish stew, but as Chick reminded me, his father never used catfish, only hand-sized, sweet Red Breast filets. The fish stew was always pronounced fit for consumption when the William Penn bottle ran dry.

Chick and I visited Mosquito Beach a year earlier on a paddle down from the Old Nichols Highway Bridge. At that time there was still a door hanging on the cabin. As Charles Mincey mentioned earlier, the door had come from the family home of Melvin Purvis, the FBI agent famous for the 1934 shootout in which the G-Men killed public enemy number one John Dillinger. Purvis had grown up in Timmonsville, knew the Gaddy family well and somehow Big Chick ended up with the door when he was salvaging building materials for the cabin. In 2013 C.P. stripped the door from the rotting frame and gave it to Chick's brother Stan who planned to clean it and keep it at his home in Florence.

At three p.m., after taking photos of all of us in front of the cabin, we mounted up and returned to the river. Along the way down to the Highway 76 Bridge we passed several homes, most of them built off Lazy River Road just above the Mincey house on Gilchrist Road. Below the houses, the forest canopy closed in again. In high water, the river splits with a channel and swamp overflow running left into the forest closer to the rear of Little Pee Dee Lodge, one of the oldest restaurants in the county. The branches come back together just above the bridge. We stayed on the right, or main channel. A year earlier the shallow water here rippled inches above a series of semi submerged cypress logs, creating waves which tossed us around as we passed through. We dubbed the place the Highway 76 rapids, but on this day five feet of water flowed smoothly over the logs.

The normally placid Little Pee Dee ripples inches above a series of semi-submerged cypress logs above the Highway 76 Bridge near Little Pee Dee Lodge.

Snowden's Landing was what we called the fishing camp on the upstream, east side of the Highway 76 Bridge at 7.2 miles downriver from Allen's Bridge. It no longer exists as a commercial boat launch, but was once a busy put in for fishermen. In the 1950s and '60s the Tom Snowden family operated Little Pee Dee Lodge, a restaurant a few hundred feet further along the highway in the direction of Nichols. The restaurant, in business since the 1920s, became one of the best-known in the county. In my youth, Tom Snowden's son Jimmy sat behind the counter in the bait shack at the landing and we bought colas and cheese crackers from him before going on the river.[17]

After the bridge, on the right, a vacant field marked by a "For Sale" sign gives no indication of its past use. Melvin Britt, often called Captain Melvin for his Navy service, once operated a grocery and fishing shop there. He was my wife Elizabeth's cousin, and had his own set of tall tales for customers. His widow eventually sold the place a few years ago and the store was razed. A developer announced he would build resort condos on the river but that didn't happen.

At low water, the remains of a naval stores barge, probably more than a century old, is outlined in the sand on the east bank opposite Captain Melvin's old business site. The barge was used to transport pine sap, once an ingredient in the manufacturing process for things like paint and varnish. In the era of the wooden ships these so-called naval stores provided pine pitch which could be mixed with fiber materials to caulk the timbers of water craft. The remains of the craft were documented with photographs for state historical authorities several years ago by my cousin Charles.

These days fly fishermen wade the shallows around the barge remains, casting for panfish. Each time I see someone with a fly rod on the river I am reminded of my Stars and Stripes colleague Norm Zeigler who has fished all over the world and written about his trips. His book *Rivers of Shadow, Rivers of Sun,* is a fine read about fishing and people, some of them friends. I'd like to bring Norm to the Little Pee Dee once and watch his graceful casts. It was his comfortable style of writing that I had in mind when trying to get down on paper our days on the river.[18]

A year earlier as I rounded a bend below the Highway 76 Bridge half a dozen turtles plopped off the trunk of a fallen oak. A lordly moccasin, with its eyes set at the front of its triangular-shaped head, lay in the sun atop the split trunk of a nearby oak. The moccasin seemed not to pay me any notice but only moments after I saw the snake it plopped off the fallen tree. This day Lin forged ahead along the same stretch so it was not clear what, if anything, had been perched along the sunny spots.

The final mile of the river before it reaches the junction with the Lumber is classic Little Pee Dee with overhanging limbs and old style river cabins on pilings close by the water. At the end of Rhode Island Road beside the river, a wild turkey flock often crosses the water in late evening. The big birds walk cautiously to the sandy river bank, then lift off with a tremendous thumping of wings to cross the 80-foot channel. They roost overnight in pine trees on the isolated spit of heavily forested land across the river.

We reached the junction of the Little Pee Dee and the Lumber eight miles downriver on the paddle. It was a Saturday afternoon and the river was filled with ski boats and high-powered bass boats. A continuous series of wakes rocked us hard as we passed a collection of the upscale homes for which The Retch is noted.

Ten minutes later and halfway down The Retch we rode one of the biggest waves into the paved boat ramp beside our house and for once didn't have to worry about trespassing or securing our valuables. Everything would be safe in our front yard beside the river. We had covered nine miles in the easiest paddle yet.

Sally Gaddy (l) and Betty Mincey, the Blanton girls from Wannamaker in Horry.

On the last day of August on the Labor Day weekend we had fried chicken and barbecue and corn on the cob and baked beans while drinking a potent wine called Red Rocket Age Reduction Elixir that my wife Elizabeth and C.P. had made the previous autumn. Before the evening was done Lin sang and played guitar for us and Aunt Betty, C.P., Aunt Sally and our neighbors Sondra and Lide Huggins.

As a five-year-old on a long flight to China Lin had listened to an hour of Hank Williams songs and never forgot the music, Chick told us. Now, as the sun set, he played and sang in a deep voice, his performance all the more interesting by the contrast of his youth and the fine features of a face that revealed the best of his mother, Hu Ye, and of his father, Chick.

The boy who speaks Mandarin also speaks country.

At eight everyone left and the house was dark save the football game on the big screen television. Two days earlier South Carolina Coach Steve Spurrier's Gamecocks had beaten North Carolina decisively 27-10 to open the season. And just after midnight, with the river alive with the wafting beach music from a party pontoon boat that floated past, Coach Dabo Swinney and his Clemson Tigers defeated number five Georgia at Death Valley 38-35.

The bills were all paid. There were no hurricanes on the storm tracker map. The Tigers and Gamecocks, or Gamecocks and Tigers, according to your preference, had started well.

The day on the river and all that followed with family and friends had been perfect.

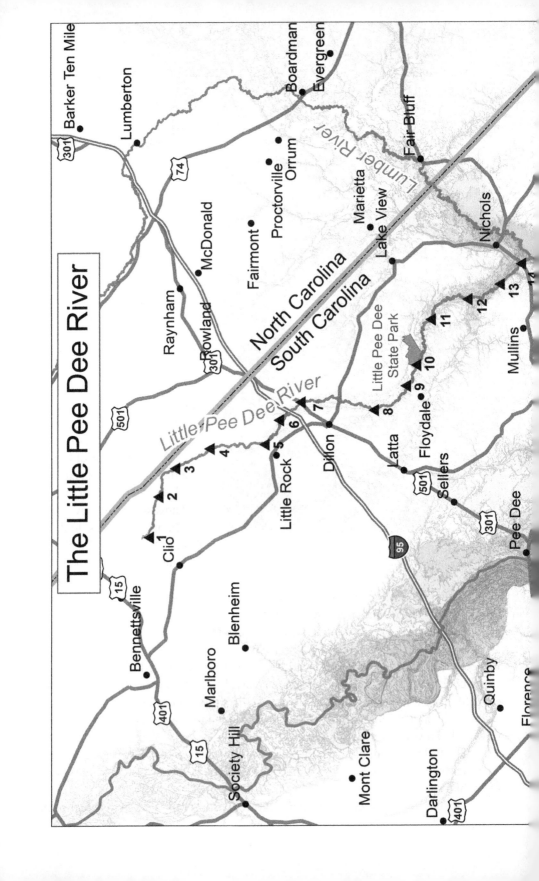

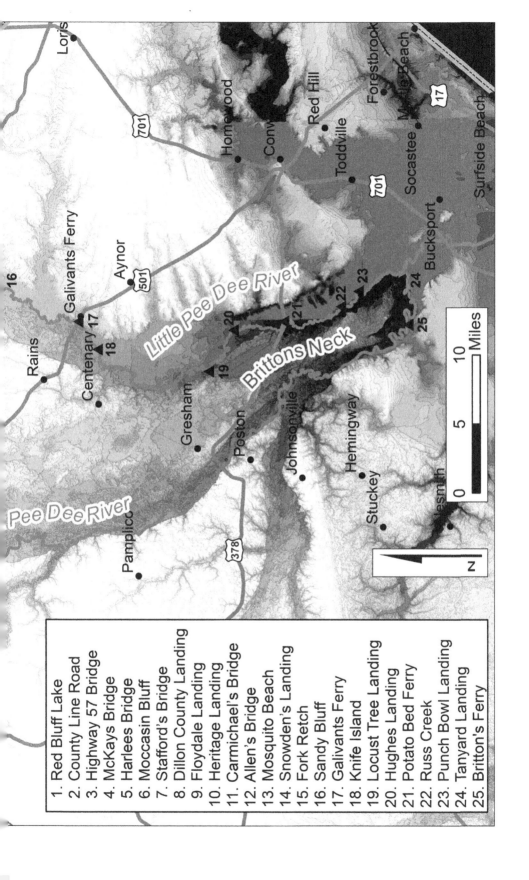

The wide water of the Little Pee Dee begins at the junction with the Lumber River.

11

Down The Wide Water On Quincey's River

Fork Retch to Galivants Ferry (16.5 Miles)

It was mid-morning, late summer. The temperature was already 85 as Chick and I straddled our kayaks in water up to our knees. In unison we fell backward into the seats and pushed away from the boat ramp below my house on Fork Retch, a mile below the junction of the Little Pee Dee and Lumber Rivers. Our destination was Galivants Ferry, 16.5 miles away with an interim stop at Sandy Bluff, six miles downriver.

We were leaving The Retch, a riverside settlement that has been called, with and without affection, the Redneck Riviera of Marion County. Average property taxes paid there are the highest in the county and it has the largest collection of year-round homes on the entire river. The word Retch, according to local legend, is a corruption of the old term reach. Fork Retch was and is a wide, straight, reach of water beyond the fork where the Little Pee Dee and Lumber Rivers join. 'I live on the river, 'I'm at The Retch' or 'I'm down at The Retch' are the typical ways residents describe the place. The houses are built along Fork Retch Court, a dead-end road that runs two miles near and along the river starting at the stop sign on U.S. 76. Cadillacs, Lincolns, Mercedes and big ticket sport utility vehicles share the highway with the usual assortment of late model Ford 150, Chevrolet Silverado and Dodge Ram pickups. Some have an oval FR sticker in the back window.

During the combination of high water and warm weather, usually April until late June and occasionally again in August-September, the mile-long, football field-wide Retch is alive with ski boats, jet skis, pontoon craft and the occasional big inlet Boston Whaler. During big boat season recreational paddlers enter the water at their own risk with the certainty they will battle wakes most of the way down this section. Saturday afternoon during high water and warm weather is probably the single worst time to transit The Retch in a paddle boat.

In late summer the water had dropped below the level required for ski boats so we shared the river with only a couple of small fishing boats. The small finger of water on the Horry side just before the bend is Rech Lake. It, like Anderson Lake on the Lumber River just above the junction, is good fishing territory. But in recent years the mudfish have begun to dominate.

Chick paddled ahead of me, energized by the fine weather. I caught up with him at the end of The Retch opposite the longest and widest sandbar on the Little Pee Dee. It measures more than 1,000 feet in length and is 100-feet wide in extreme low water. Two of the houses on the shore have piers out to the low water level, just like on the coastal inlets.

The Little Pee Dee is a relatively shallow river along its 109 mile length with an average depth of about five feet. It descends gradually 190 feet before it reaches the Great Pee Dee. It is considered navigable by the Army Corps of Engineers for the last 99 miles although Fork Retch at Mile Marker 58 has always been the upriver limit for larger craft. In extreme low water the main flow down The Retch is less than a foot deep. But here, at the big sandbar the extremes of the river face each other. The bottom of the river at the undercut bank on the Horry side is one of the deepest on the river. Water depth can be 15 or more feet in flood stage and the bottom was still six-feet down on this morning.

Wealth, or the lack of it, turned out to be the morning topic as we hugged the east bank and its cool shadows. Chick and I chose professions not known for big money. We talked of friends who were millionaires and multimillionaires and how they had gotten rich. We decided most of them weren't particularly happy and finished the standard rationalization by agreeing we had both done what we wanted to do from a fairly young age. Any other conclusion such as the suggestion that we had just stumbled along in professions that appeared out of thin air would have

A classic Little Pee white sandbar extends around a bend below Fork Retch.

given us cause to feel unhappy about life. And that would have been unfortunate, given how happy we were at the moment on the river. We did agree that as seniors we would be willing to go back and determine if big money and big misery are fellow travelers.

I did, however, check my wallet when I got home and found it stuffed with a twenty, a five and a one dollar bill. In addition I was carrying a coupon for a cheap Thickburger® at Hardees and a 20 percent discount certificate for Harbor Freight. The casual observer might conclude my finances were as shaky as that of the U.S. Government. I knew differently: I didn't owe any of my $26 to China.

A distracting rustle in the top branches of a big pine alongside the river interrupted our conversation. I back paddled until the black body of a Turkey Vulture was clearly outlined between gray Spanish moss and the green boughs of a loblolly pine. The vulture had us under observation. Even from 50 feet away we could clearly see the bald red head and hooked beak of what most people call a buzzard.

"That is *Cathartes aura*," Chick said. The vulture exhibits a sinister appearance in comparison with wild turkeys which have a paler, almost pink head. The Wild Turkey, *Meleagris gallopavo*, is usually smaller than a turkey vulture and the male turkey has a fleshy wattle or snood that hangs from its beak. Turkeys along the river bank are there to cross and do so in a loud, thumping flight that rarely reaches more than 50 feet above the water. The vulture is one of nature's most accomplished flyers, lifting off smoothly and usually soaring without apparent effort far above the water until a potential meal is spotted.

A Turkey Vulture cruises above the Little Pee Dee Swamp in search of a meal.

Chick told me about an experiment he made years earlier in a farm field with numerous roosting vultures nearby. Some vultures feed only on carrion, dead meat. Others will start eating dying animals. He lay out in a field on his back with a hat over his head and watched the vultures circle. They primarily use their finely tuned sense of smell to detect decaying flesh but he thought he would test their eyesight. A few of the big vultures circled a thousand feet up but none ever came down any closer to inspect what would have been a more than substantial meal.

"I know, it sounds crazy," Chick said.

I agreed.

Vultures and turkeys are frequently seen along this stretch of river. The vultures scavenge the swamps by circling above, riding thermals, using sharp eyes and a keen sense of smell to find dead animals. The turkeys feed in farm fields near the river and find sanctuary in the trees at night. The reintroduction of turkeys has been a chapter in the rewilding of the Little Pee Dee in my lifetime. It is the wild game bird of South Carolina, but had almost died out in the river basin because of over hunting in the first half of the 20th century. Restocking by state wildlife officials has been highly successful and there are several flocks along The Retch and dozens more up and down the river.

Shep McKenzie Road, just below the big sandbar that marks the end of The Retch, is probably the most scenic river road in Marion County. It turns off Fork Retch Court opposite the county boat landing and cuts through the swamp to the river, where it runs for more than 1,000 feet alongside the water. When the river nears flood stage the dirt road is inundated, shutting off traffic to the next paved road, Grice's Ferry Court. McKenzie Road is a favorite walking trail for local residents and also a lunchtime stop for many who purchase a fast food meal in Mullins. Unfortunately, those who come down to the river to eat often leave a trail of french fry containers, hamburger cartons and paper cups that blight the beauty of this tree-shaded road.

Willie Mae Hicks of Marion fishes along Shep McKenzie road.

Grice's Ferry Court Road fronts a dozen or so river houses spaced along a quarter-mile section of the river. From there it is another mile to a settlement called Red Bluff, not to be confused with Red Bluff settlement and lake on the upper river in Marlboro County. Red Bluff in Marion County has a collection of houses and trailers built alongside and near the river. It is a good landing for fishing boats. State road S-34-593, which connects to the Old Mullins Road, leads down to Red Bluff.[19]

The section of the Little Pee Dee from the U.S. Highway 76 bridge at Snowden's Landing above The Retch all the way down to Red Bluff is an exception to the relatively unspoiled look of the river. After Red Bluff nature again gains the ascendancy with natural forest on each side and an abundance of birds, beavers, an occasional otter, and plenty of snakes and turtles.

The land along the east bank of the river is part of the Little Pee Dee Heritage Preserve/Wildlife Management area, which began above The Retch on the Lumber River. The Heritage Preserve covers over 10,000 acres with 38.5 miles along the Lumber and the Little Pee Dee down to Gunter Lake in Lower Marion County.[20]

A quarter of a mile downriver from Red Bluff, Chick swung his kayak left into a wide opening and we entered a slough leading into the swamp. Our progress up the narrow channel was accompanied by the steady plopping sounds of turtles unceremoniously abandoning sun-drenched logs for the water and the kerplunks of snakes dropping into the water. A good-sized moccasin literally fell from the trunk of a fallen tree and we passed within eight feet of the ripples. In the slough we found the remains of a double row of creosote pilings. Spikes had once been driven into the top of the pilings and now were rusting reminders of the fasteners that we guessed had held the framework for a temporary narrow gauge railroad bridge erected to roll timber from the swamp to the river.

On the inside of the next bend we entered a second slough and also paddled it to the end. Turtles again regularly dropped into the water in front of us and Chick turned and followed a large water snake crossing open water. It escaped into a clump of bushes between cypress knees.

One mile further downstream we entered an oxbow on the Marion County side. After a few feet our kayaks hit sand and we were forced to monkey walk with our hands pushing our craft across the bottom. Finally, even that failed and we got out and walked the sandy shallows, letting the kayaks drift in front of us until the water was deep enough to mount up again. We were preceded into the oxbow by a Great Blue Heron, which skillfully fished the shallows while keeping a wary eye on us. Eventually the bird exited, circled around and began fishing behind us.

At one point deep in the oxbow we photographed a massive cypress knee that measured at least eight feet high. And opposite the big cypress knee, the inner sandbar had sprouted a heavy patch of southern wild rice which grows from April to September along the river. It is an aquatic grass plant that is a favorite of ducks, Chick explained. The Latin is *Zizaniopsis milaceae* and it can grow to 12 feet, he said. It is monoecious, which means that it has male and female flowers on the same stems.

The oxbow exit had silted up with white sand and the only direct water pathway back out to the river was under the branches of several trees. Chick pointed out big wasp nests up in the boughs but decided to go through.

"Dive out of the boat and get under the water if they come after you," he said.

"How?" I asked. "The water is six inches deep. They would sting anything sticking up and there would be a lot of you and me above water."

He didn't respond, lowered his head and pushed through the opening.

"Nothing to it," he said when he came out the other side.

I declined to follow and found a pathway around the branches. With a little monkey walking I slid my kayak across the sand and also exited the oxbow unscathed.

Mitch Abernethy and his son Brown of Lincolnton, N.C., push through alligator weed on an oxbow below Fork Retch.

The river forks on the first bend beyond the oxbow. What had once been a little cut-through was now the narrow main channel. The old river to the right was still wide and we went that way, skirting the west side of a wooded island created when the river split. A few minutes later we floated past a modern home on a sand hill bank fronted by a protective growth of cypress knees. The river was only a few inches deep there and in another ten years the channel will probably dry up completely in low water.

We heard road traffic from the S.C. Highway 917 Bridge as we approached the main channel and moments later spotted the road crossing where workers were widening the bridge. We passed under the bridge and pulled in at the Sandy Bluff Landing on the Horry side.

Remembering Quincey Strickland

Joan Strickland of Sandy Bluff Landing shows family photos including a picture of her late husband Quincey.

Joan Ham Strickland, 78, lives in the second house down from the landing. A lifetime earlier, when she was 12, a boy rode to her farm house in Horry County on a bicycle and delivered a valentine. The 14-year-old, Quincey, signed it 'to my sweetheart' and she hid it from her grandfather for fear he would be upset. But he found it and read it and told her, "That boy will make you a good husband someday." Later, when she underwent an appendectomy at Mullins Hospital, Quincey rode his bike 10 miles on dirt roads from Ketchuptown in Horry to visit her. They went to the Junior-Senior at Floyds High School when she was an eighth grader and he was a junior. And married when he left Clemson after one semester, lonesome for her. She was 15. They began a happy rural life in Horry and eventually had four children, two boys, two girls.

Quincey farmed for a while, then went to work in a plant at Sellers in Marion County. Joan went back to school and became a nurse. They bought the little, brown cottage down from Sandy Bluff Landing in 1986 and filled a wall in the place with a collection of family pictures that would eventually include nine grandchildren. It was from the cottage that Joan and Quincey set out to cross the river in April 2003 in their Jon boat. Quincey thought he might have a big catfish on one of the lines he had set on the far side.

"Two weeks earlier he had won a fishing contest at Nichols with a 69-pound flathead catfish from the Little Pee Dee," Joan recalled. "And when we got across the river I could see we had a big fish on one of the lines. Quincey tried to bring the fish in and Joan felt the boat rock. She turned to see her husband of 52 years sliding over the side. She tried to pull him in, but could not. He told her he would be okay in the water as he held to some branches near the bank. Joan decided the only thing she could do was get help. The boat motor would not crank and she paddled as hard as she could across the river where two men answered her call for help.

Quincey was lifeless when they returned, but they managed to get him in the boat and recrossed the river to the landing. The Horry County Coroner came, but decided the case was not in his jurisdiction. "Although the body was on the Horry side, he said the death had occurred on the Marion side," Joan remembered. "So everyone had to wait for the Marion County Coroner to come to the Horry side."

While they were waiting a game warden arrived to also investigate and a crowd gathered. Amid the confusion, the big catfish disappeared.

"As a nurse, I knew he was gone," Joan said. "They said at first he drowned but I knew what had happened. He had had a mild stroke ten years before and he decided he didn't want anyone to try and resuscitate him if something like that happened again." An autopsy showed Quincey had suffered a cerebral hemorrhage.

Nearly 11 years after that day on the river Joan Strickland still lives in their home. "I feel like I'm close to Quincey here," she said in late 2013, two days before what would have been their 63rd wedding anniversary. She still sleeps in the bedroom they made out of the front porch. "When he was alive it was just screened in and we slept there year round," she said. "We used an electric blanket in the winter and put plastic over the covers when it rained."

She has since walled in the porch but there is always a view of the Little Pee Dee through the big windows. A view of Quincey's River.

When Chick and I came ashore at Sandy Bluff our trusty driver C.P. was waiting. For once he told us stories instead of listening. His father had built a cabin not far downriver from the bridge in 1944, he said. He wanted Chick to see it the next time we were on the river. Two months earlier he and I had put in at Sandy Bluff for a visit to the cabin which is now on his son Ken's 1,000 acre tract along the Horry side. That day we rode in the Betty Boat, a beat-up old fiberglass fishing and ski boat my uncle claims he gave my Aunt Betty as a birthday present many years before. The boat became a standing family joke because our aunt had never driven the boat and rarely rode in it.

We pulled up into a narrow slough about a mile down river and the cabin was at the end of a short walk through the trees. It is a simple, one-room structure with no running water, not even an outhouse. My uncle had brought some covering material and began work on a rotted out chair bottom. I wandered around and finally looked in the cabin where I found a water moccasin on the floor and finished it off with a rock when it would not come out from behind a bunk bed.

I came back outside and asked my uncle how he felt about snakes.

"They don't worry me," he said.

Years ago he was bitten by a venomous copperhead while working on his farm. "It just hurt a little," he said.

It took him about half an hour to recover the chair bottom. He could have easily purchased a replacement chair for a few dollars. That would, however, not have fit the philosophy of his generation, my father's generation. They became adults in the Great Depression. Waste not, want not became a lifetime habit.

Betty and C.P. Mincey built a successful and happy life together on a farm along the Little Pee Dee.

C.P. and Betty lived in a log cabin without indoor plumbing when he came back from U.S. Navy service in World War II. "We were as poor as church mice," he said. "I bought a car, but I couldn't make the payments and sold it. Then I got a bicycle and rode it to work at the barber shop in Nichols and back. If Betty had to go somewhere I let her have the bicycle. I never bought another car that I didn't pay cash for." He cut hair for 50 cents a head in his little barber shop in downtown Nichols, just north of where the Lumber and Pee Dee join, for more than a quarter century. On Saturdays as many as 100 men and boys would sit down in his chair, the same one he now has in the corner of the kitchen at his farm. He saved his money and did well, eventually buying a farm, a beach house, more farms and all the while ensuring a good life for his family. Aunt Betty ran the house, raised three children who all became college graduates and in her spare time cut the grass, kept the books and paid the bills.

To this day my uncle, who is most definitely well-to-do, feels he must demonstrate frugality, always living modestly. His advice to his grandchildren: "If you're doing well, keep it to yourself. Your family will already know it and your friends won't care. But the people that don't like you will like you even less." Second to my father, he has been the best mentor I've known. And he is among the smartest people I've known. His basic philosophy is rock solid—work hard every day, save your money, invest wisely, particularly in real estate and farms, be a good person in every way possible, worship on Sunday, help people who need it, care for the land and don't forget to have fun. And always have a new project that requires your attention and hard work. When you stop moving you start dying, he will tell you.

Later in life when Aunt Betty, once a fierce teetotaler like my mother, broadened her thoughts on alcohol, the family health regimen began to include a drink of wine or moonshine before bed. That's when he began making his own wine with labels like Red Rocket and also got hold of some potent moonshine and mixed it with apple juice yielding his own 'Apple Pie' mixture subtly potent enough to require filing a flight plan before the first drink.

"You sleep a whole lot better after a little drink or two," he explained one night while mixing white lightning and honey." I should add I've never seen him even slightly inebriated.

My father had to quit school after the sixth grade to work during the Great Depression. C.P., who was several years younger than my dad, said he somehow got to the 12th grade but was certain he would never graduate from Floyds High School at Duford in Horry County. "I failed the second grade," he said. "And when I got to be a senior I knew there just wasn't any way I could pass English. But my best friend, James Colon Grainger, who had graduated from Floyds the previous year, was dating the English teacher. I told him he had to do something to get me through. So he did something. I still don't know what it was. But I passed with a 70, the minimum. I became a high school graduate." The diploma must have raised his intelligence, he said. Because a while later he had the good sense to marry Betty Blanton who had been class valedictorian the year after he graduated. Her sister Clarice, my mother, had been valedictorian four years earlier.

Sandy Bluff to Galivants Ferry

Chick and I returned to Sandy Bluff Landing a month later. It was low water but the river still measured almost 400 feet across. It would remain wide for much of the remainder of our water journey. Our destination was Galivants Ferry, eight miles downriver, where U.S. Highway 501, a four-lane main traffic artery to Myrtle Beach, crosses the river.

This day, Chick and I stopped a mile downriver at the old cabin on Ken's farm. I stayed in the kayak and kept an eye out for a moccasin that slid into the water about fifteen feet away. It did not reappear until Chick returned. This time it dropped in from a stump about 10-feet to my left. Since Chick and I visited, the entire cabin has been taken apart and moved across a slough to a location closer to the river. Master carpenter Lee Grant Page, who rebuilt our deck on the river at Fork Retch, led the work and reassembled the building.[21]

Sandy Bluff to Galivants Ferry turned out to be an uncomplicated cruise through a classic cypress swamp forest. We pointed the kayaks downriver and for the most part made only slight corrections with the paddles to stay lined up with the flow. If we got our bows pointed correctly, we could enter the cut bank side of a bend and use the fast-flowing water to slingshot our kayaks on a line toward the next cut bank. Anytime we wanted to slow our pace, we drifted to the inside of the bend, the sandbar side, and floated across a few inches of golden-colored water

Master carpenter Lee Grant Page led the reassembly work on the 1944 cabin built by C.P. Mincey's father.

until our hulls dragged the bottom.

The Horry County side from the S.C. Highway 917 Bridge down to the bend nearest Gator Lake on the Marion side, features brilliant white sandhills beginning at the water and stretching back into the undergrowth. The pure white sand spread on these ridges can easily be observed on aerial imagery of the Little Pee Dee region. We passed a number of old arms of the river, now lakes, which flank both sides. On the Marion County side these lakes——Home, Jack, Cypress, Smokey, Gator and Bass—are closest to the dirt road that leads to the settlement of houses around the public boat launch at Cartwheel Landing, 5.5 miles downriver from Sandy Bluff. The Horry County lakes—White Oak, Gerald, Scrogging, Hughes, Vaught, Timber, Broad—are scattered in the river vegetation belt almost all the way down to Galivants Ferry.

We reached Cartwheel Landing in early afternoon on what had become a perfect day; the temperature had climbed to eighty, a light breeze wafted mostly with us and the current moved us along with almost no paddling effort on our part. About five miles remained to Galivants Ferry.

The second half of the trip down from Sandy Bluff was a mirror of the first. At one point Chick found a fallen tree curved over a stretch of the water and steered directly at it, halting under the arch. This was such a piece of cake, nothing like the upper river, he reminded me, until the current shoved him sideways momentarily, threating to flip his kayak.

"Uh, oh," he yelled and barely got out of the predicament by retreating upstream.

Perhaps some unseen force had had the wisdom to remind us of the obvious. No matter the season or the water level, the river remains in charge. Overconfidence will get you wet and extreme overconfidence can get you drowned.

A few minutes later we found the perfect sandbar and spread out a feast of turkey sandwiches, ice-cold water, pistachio nuts and candy bars. We gorged ourselves while lying back on the sand with our kayaks for support. This was our easiest day on the river yet. A day to observe, watch the wildlife and take time to enjoy the privilege of being alive and outside and learning.

C.P. said he would be waiting at the Galivants Ferry Landing when we arrived and we heard, then saw his trusty Ford 250 diesel pick-up moments after we paddled into the Marion County boat landing on the downstream side of the bridge. He was in a fine mood with plenty of energy and once we had stacked and tied the kayaks in the back of the pickup he tapped the accelerator briskly and we sped up the incline to Highway 501. The truck tires chirped as we headed for the bridge with a long line of beach traffic closing in at high speed a few hundred yards behind.

Wham!

That was the sound I heard first and when I looked back my orange kayak was sliding past Chick's kayak out of the bed of the truck onto the highway directly into the path of at least a dozen cars and SUVs. It skidded right and left on the pavement, trailing the broken tie down rope. Fine shavings of orange colored plastic marked the trail of the kayak. It came to rest in a few seconds upright and broadside to the oncoming vehicles. C.P., ignoring the traffic, slammed on the brakes in the middle of the right lane and waited for us to get the kayak, or what was left of it, back in the truck.

Luckily the first couple of drivers braked immediately and moved over to the left lane to get past. The other cars had time to stop and waited patiently as Chick and I hustled the craft into the truck atop his kayak. We jumped in and drove across the bridge to the Exxon Station where a closer examination revealed a lot of scarred plastic on the bottom, particularly the keel. But nothing appeared to be broken.

"How was the trip?" C.P. asked when we got back in. He passed right over the drama at the bridge. So we ignored it too and told him about our day, pleased that he wanted to know all the details. He now has artificial hips that make it hard to get into small boats, so we knew most of his river experiences in recent years had been vicarious. In making our report we engaged in the time-honored family tradition of embellishment: The snakes got bigger and closer, the fallen trees became massive timbers, the current into some coves swift and the natural beauty mindboggling. Our uncle is a smart fellow, smarter than both of us combined on a lot of levels, so he sifted through the exaggeration, aware from personal experience, however, that our biggest claim was true.

It had been another beautiful ride.

In the wide, shallow water below Galivants Ferry in late summer the white sand bottom appears golden as far as the eye can see.

12

Knife Island, Ex In-laws And A *Nerodia sipedon*

Galivants Ferry to Locust Tree Landing (14.5 Miles)

We returned to Galivants Ferry with some trepidation because the last time we were here two weeks earlier my kayak fell off the truck and skidded down the center of Highway 501 with about 100 cars bearing down hard on it. It survived with a few scratches and didn't show any leaks as we pushed off from the Marion County Landing on a hot summer morning and glided past the depth marker in the middle of the river. The marker is the official water level for the Lower Little Pee Dee[22] and it showed less than five feet. That meant low water along the nearly 15-mile section down to Locust Tree landing.

In colonial times, Galivants Ferry was the gateway from Liberty County, now called Marion, to Kingston County, now called Horry. The crossing was first mentioned as Elirsee's Landing in 1792 and operated by boatman Richard Gallevan whose name morphed into Galivants Ferry.[23]

A short distance west on U.S. Highway 501 a marker commemorates Francis Marion's important victory against a large band of Tory militia in the Battle of the Blue Savannah on Sept. 4, 1780. In typical Marion fashion, despite commanding only 52 troops, he confronted a superior force of 200 men led by local Tory leaders Maj. Micajah Ganey and Capt. Jesse Barefield (Barfield).[24] Maj. John James, leading Marion's advance guard, met the Tory advance on the road through the scrub oak not too far from present day Ariels Crossroad where S.C. Highway 41 crosses over U.S. 501. After a wild chase, the Tories initially fled into the swamp in front of James' charge. From prisoners Marion learned the location of the reassembled Tory force and attacked again. In the face of a force at least five times his own, Marion feigned retreat and the Tories followed, riding into an ambush on the edge of the Little Pee Dee Swamp. When the shooting ended after the second engagement, Ganey and Barefield's men fled into the swamp in defeat, much as Marion's men often did after victory.

A marker near the Little Pee River gives the history of the Galivants Ferry Stump Meeting.

Professor Robert Bass in his book *Swamp Fox* wrote, "Next morning Marion sent a patrol back to the Blue Savannah. After riding over the battlegrounds, they returned with a report that during the night the Loyalists had crawled out of the swamp and slunk off to their cabins. In two skirmishes, at a cost of having four men wounded and two horses killed, he had broken the power of the Tories east of the Pee Dee."[25]

In 1876 gubernatorial candidate and former Confederate General Wade Hampton, promoted his campaign with a so-called stump speech near the Galivants Ferry landing. Over the years the political rally here with speeches became a state Democratic Party tradition which has continued into the 21st century. In the beginning the candidates reputedly stood on tree stumps to enable the crowd to better see and hear them.[26]

The Holliday family came to Galivants Ferry after the Civil War and eventually built one of the largest agricultural enterprises in the state. J.W. Holliday opened a store near the river in 1869 and branched out into farming and other business pursuits. His son George J. Holliday grew the business and introduced large scale tobacco farming to the area in the early 20th century. The Holliday operation is now called Pee Dee Farms and still has extensive holdings in the area.[27]

On this morning, a Barred Owl sounded in the distance and Chick cupped his hands around his mouth and called back—who who – who, who, who – letting his tone rise on the final note. A hawk circled overhead and egrets fished the shallows behind a grass-covered spit of white sand along one edge in the river. A Wood Duck, the first of several we saw during the day, flushed and beat a loud retreat across the shallows.

We floated around a bend and onto a straight where the entire river, bank to bank, seemed no more than six inches deep. The dark water flowed over a massive expanse of dazzling white bottom sand, creating the image of a mirror-like golden-hued bottom that stretched as far downriver as we could see. The river along this section averages 200 feet across and the green belt it flows through is a mile and a half wide at most points. On the Horry side someone had taken a great deal of effort to climb a tree along the bank and nail up a spiritual admonition. The sign, tacked 20 feet up a pine, reminded river travelers "You Are Lost Without Jesus."

We glided lazily downriver, content travelers between the gold below and the brilliant, cloudless, azure sky above. We reached Huggins Landing on the Horry side in an hour, and then minutes later Carmichael Lake on the Marion side. The lake extends from the river for a third of a mile and we turned in to see what it was like. Fish, probably Muds, broke the water regularly as we glided under the shadowy canopy of the cypresses along the water's edge. In the cool, under the trees, we smeared on sunscreen and adjusted bandanas to cover our necks from the sun.

On the river again, we began to encounter fallen trees and the roots and broken trunks of trees that had toppled into the river over the years. But the obstacles that would have been near impassable on the upper river were merely slight hindrances here, easily avoided with a few flicks of the paddle to slide left or right in the broad channel.

Ninety minutes downriver we rounded a bend and came upon three large deer drinking from the river. Deer normally prefer partially hidden openings where they can drink without being seen except from directly across the river. But there they were, standing on the point of a sandbar a good 50 yards in the open with their heads down. We snapped away furiously with our cameras and got perhaps a dozen shots before we were sighted and the deer bounded across the sand and into the woods.

The Little Pee Dee forked a quarter mile below Carmichael Lake. The left channel, an old course of the river, flowed to the east of Knife Island. We took the west channel that went past the landing. A lone fisherman in a small electric-powered boat had anchored on the next bend. He cast a spinning rod outfitted with a red and white bobber and worms on a hook. His boat sat atop a bed of lily pads and before we passed he pulled in a large bream.

"Having any luck?" I asked.

Two deer flee from the water's edge after being surprised while drinking on an open sandbar below Galivants Ferry.

"Not really," he answered and turned away to watch the bobber being pulled under again.

We had been on the river a little over two hours when we floated alongside the first of the houses at Knife Island Landing, four miles down from Galivants Ferry on the Marion County side. We could see perhaps a dozen houses along or near the water and more on interior roads.

Five women were in the water, sunbathing in half-submerged beach chairs on a sandbar below a large river house. One called out, "Where are you coming from?"

Chick stopped to answer and found he knew one of the women. She was Suzanne Baker, sister of his first wife, Holly. He hadn't seen her in more than 20 years, but they had parted on good terms and resumed family discussions as if there had been no interruption. Her husband George was in the area, she said, and she knew he would like to see Chick. We stuck around for a few more minutes but finally pushed off again when George didn't show.

Twenty minutes later we rounded a bend and were confronted by a line of tree trunks and root debris that for the first time on this stretch blocked direct passage down the river. We faced a low-water version of what we had seen countless times upriver during flood stage. An oak trunk, its limbs bare of leaves, blocked most of the main channel. To the left, on the Horry County side, additional partially submerged fallen trees closed off the rest of the river. We stepped out and let the kayaks float down to the smaller trees. When we caught up, it was a simple matter to lift our craft over the obstacles and mount them again in the free flowing river below.

Even the wide water below Galivants Ferry becomes difficult at times when the river level drops, exposing fallen trees and other debris.

Shortly afterwards we rounded another bend and heard the sound of a motor in the swamp. The mechanical rattle reverberated in the trees like a cross between a chain saw and an outboard. Seconds later a green Outlander Max all-terrain vehicle emerged from the woods at speed and raced along the bank until it was parallel with us. The rider waved us over. Chick's former brother-in-law George Baker proceeded to catch him up on family events in the decades since the divorce.

Twenty minutes later we pushed off again and a mile and a half further downriver reached Davis Landing, a settlement of eight or nine houses, also on the Marion County side. Davis Landing and Knife Island Landing are reached off Davis Landing Court Road which branches from S.C.Highway 41, two-tenths of a mile north of Creek Bridge High School.

The Davis family once ran a large agricultural operation in this area of Lower Marion County. The old company store and outbuildings stand deserted along a dirt road just off Highway 41, nine-tenths of a mile east of the intersection where 41 and 41A join below Centenary. Jim Davis, who still manages the family land, is a soft-spoken man with an encyclopedic knowledge of area history. He now lives in Marion but his sister Ann Earle Lane has a home a few hundred feet from the old company store opposite a small farm I bought from their cousin several years ago. Earlier in the year Jim drove me down past the old company store on No Name Road to Carey Lake, a secluded, hook-shaped body of water deep in the swamp forest. It is typical of the lakes along this stretch of the river, nearly all of them part of former river channels.

Cypress Creek Lake, below Carey Lake, is on the Marion Side, only 200 feet from the main course of the river. And a half mile below Cypress Creek, Palmer Lake curves for almost half a mile, roughly paralleling the river. On the Horry County side, a similar series of small lakes parallel the path of the river. They include Liza Lake, Barnett Lake, Pigpen Lakes, Jack Lake, Kinney Lake, Little Barnett Lake and Round Lake. The longest of them is Sandy Isle Lake, stretching a half mile and almost directly opposite Carey. The last of the lakes on the Horry side is Newfound Lake which is east of the last bend before reaching Locust Tree Court Landing.

We were now officially in Lower Marion County, where the river swamp and adjoining forest were alive with game including the scourge of local farmers, feral hogs. The hogs root up large areas at will, often damaging crops. Jim Davis showed me a big cage trap where hunters had captured a 250-pound hog earlier in the year. On my farm, which is more than a mile from the river near Centenary, these wild pigs wander the swamp foraging for food. They root up large areas near and in corn and peanut fields. There is no closed season on feral hogs; they can be hunted at any time.

On the river we passed a sandbar where an abandoned cabin was built on blocks near the water. Sipirs Surar Shak was stenciled in ragged white letters above the door. Perhaps it had been Sugar Shak before the paint faded. The cabin had guy wires attached to the foundation and what appeared to be an official permit nailed to the front wall, meaning it could have been a house boat with hidden floats underneath.

Three miles above Locust Tree we slowed to look at Palmer Lake through the trees on the Marion side. It is the most interesting of the old river arms. But in the low water we didn't see a good way through. The river split 15 minutes below Palmer Lake and I went left while Chick took the right fork. The wooded area in the middle was hardly longer and wider than a football field and we came back together five minutes later. Chick reported on an interesting fern he photographed. I found a good place to camp on the east side of the little island and marked it on the map for future reference. Anytime Chick lagged behind I knew he was probably taking pictures of ferns. He is an expert on this subject also. His book, *Ferns of the West Indies*, was published at mid-year in 2013.[28]

The shadows were lengthening as we turned away from the river into the narrow entry to Locust Tree Landing at 7:30. A dozen or so homes have been built alongside the dirt road leading to the landing. But there was no one in sight, either at the landing or at any of the houses. We called C.P. and he said he was driving around somewhere out on S.C. Highway 908, a cut-through road off S.C. 41 leading to Highway 378. He couldn't find the entrance road and had never been to that part of the county, he said. It was for us a surprising admission on his part. We had assumed there wasn't a place in Marion County he hadn't been at least once in his 87 years.

A large Northern Water snake attempts to swallow a catfish at Locust Tree Landing.

As we stood waiting for our ride, we heard splashing against the sandy bank of the small island that separates Locust Tree Landing from the river. There, in the shallows, a snake was swallowing a large catfish whole. The fish would not go down and the snake writhed with its unhinged jaw stretched to the limit. The large white belly of the catfish flopped left and right on the water as the snake, which we thought was a water moccasin, tried to get the fish down head first. After ten minutes or so, the snake, with fish in tow, moved from the bank and swam into the brush on our side, not six feet away. We could still see the white belly of the fish as it moved in the shadows. I took pictures and at the time the snake seemed small, but when I got back and input them into my computer the body shown on my monitor was large, as big as a muscular arm. We estimated the fish must have been between three and five pounds. I was convinced the snake was a water moccasin. Chick said it might be a banded water snake which has similar coloring. He sent the pictures to his friend, biology professor Dr. Michael Dorcas at Davidson College. A few days later Dr. Dorcas reported that the snake "looks like a *Nerodia sipedon*, certainly not a cmouth."

Chick translated the professor's comment. "It is the Northern or Midland Water Snake," he said. A few days after the identification, Chick messaged me. "In the Piedmont this week," he reported. "Staying in Walhalla and walking a ten mile long power line route. Doing about three miles a day. Rained this morning and this afternoon. Soaked all day and had to ford a 4 foot deep creek. Saw a giant *Nerodia sipedon*, probably a Northern Water Snake…Moves like a copperhead and is very copper-colored. Tracked him down for a photo and almost stepped on him. He shot between my legs and made no attempt to strike. He was moving too fast to photograph. More of the same tomorrow."

As the sun set we heard the familiar rumble of C.P.'s Ford diesel and moments later saw the truck bumping hard across the ruts at speed trailing a cloud of dust. Seconds later our octogenarian uncle sprightly climbed out of the truck. He wore ragged Bermudas, a t-shirt and a battered Farm Bureau hat. He had dismounted his John Deere tractor in the field and driven straight to us not long after the pickup call came, he said.

"What'd you see today?" he asked.

"A lot," I answered.

On the 40-minute ride home Chick gave him the appropriately embellished highlights.

Brilliant sunshine highlights a home built on the shoreline of Gunter Lake below Locust Tree Landing.

13

Pity The Foreigners At Hughes Landing

Locust Tree Landing to Potato Bed Ferry (17 Miles)

Today's paddle would take us down through the Britton's Neck[29] community of Revolutionary War note and along some of the most beautiful and isolated stretches of the Little Pee Dee in Lower Marion County. Our destination was Potato Bed Ferry, a landing at the U.S. Highway 378 Bridge near Johnsonville, nearly 17 miles downriver from Locust Tree.

Water levels had risen more than two feet in the two weeks since we had last been on the river. Our arms and shoulders were loose and we were sweating profusely in the late summer morning heat by the time we covered the 2.3 miles to Gunter Lake, a half-mile long stretch of water reaching north into the swamp on the Horry side. It is accessed by road from Old Pee Dee Highway at Galivants Ferry onto Gunter Island Road.

Along the upper shore of Gunter Lake shortly after the entrance we found an unusual bald cypress, shorter than many of the older trees but with a massive base that resembled a horse's hoof. Chick speculated the tree, *Taxodium distichum,* was old enough to have been a landmark for Indians traveling the river four hundred years earlier. The oldest known living cypress tree has been on the planet for more than 2,000 years, Chick pointed out.[30]

We paddled against the wind going up the lake for a few minutes before turning back to the river. Upon entering the channel, we found the wind had shifted and was still in our faces. That happens as often on the river as in flying where you seem to have a headwind going and returning on trips. In the next bend we glided past a waterside settlement of two dozen or so houses, 2.5 miles downriver. The houses were built near Black Island Road, which runs into Gunter Island Road and eventually Pee Dee Road South. After the houses, we entered one of the most unspoiled stretches we had encountered on the lower river. We passed Little Cane Island and Big Cane Island on the Marion side before reaching a white sand bank that marked the boundary of Indigo Island on the Horry side. A look at satellite photos later revealed we had come alongside an immense white sand ridge that ran near the river for almost three miles.

The indigo plant, and the dye it produced, was an important crop in 18th century South Carolina. Before the Civil War the export of indigo was second in value to rice in the state, thanks in great measure to the pioneering work of Eliza Lucas, a young woman credited with being the first person to cultivate indigo in North America. Her father, a career British officer, left her to run his plantations in the Charleston area, and she did so from the age of 16, also experimenting with the cultivation of flax, hemp and silk. Eliza Lucas later married distinguished South Carolina landowner Charles Pinckney. Their sons Thomas and Charles Cotesworth fought in the Revolutionary War and then served the new nation with distinction afterwards. Charles Cotesworth Pinckney and his second cousin Charles Pinckney were signers of the U.S. Constitution. When Eliza Lucas Pinckney died in 1793 President George Washington was one of the pallbearers at her funeral in Philadelphia.[31]

Two and a half hours out, somewhere alongside the ridge identified as Indigo Island, we rechecked the maps and Chick discovered that two of the six sections he had copied the previous night were on a different scale than the others. That meant an extra hour on the water.

We had hoped to reach Potato Bed Ferry, where we had left his car that morning, by six. That arrival time was now in doubt. We definitely wanted to make it in before dark just after eight-thirty although we were prepared to spend the night on the river.

We passed a house trailer with a manicured grass lawn, then an expansive river house on concrete block supports. Half an hour afterwards we floated past the houses at the end of White Oak Road in Britton's Neck. Another fine river house, elevated on cross-braced wooden beams, surely provided an impressive view of the river bend. The big house was followed shortly afterwards by a smaller one with a collapsed roof and a for sale sign.

On the river we were less than two miles from S.C. Highway 908 which passes through Britton's Neck Community on the way to its intersection with U.S. Highway 378. We were deep in the territory that had served as a primary movement and escape area for Francis Marion and his men. They rode the long neck of land between the rivers toward the ferry on the Great Pee Dee run by the Britton family. Once across the river they settled into their camp on Snow Island in what is now Florence County.

It was in a wide turn near White Oak that an aluminum V-hull boat mounted with a big outboard and driven by a man who went out of his way not to look in our direction, passed doing at least 50 mph. He sped past a Department of Natural Resources notice that cautioned: SLOW. YOU ARE RESPONSIBLE FOR YOUR WAKE.

A little over a mile further, alongside the outlet at Martin's Lodge Ct., seven and a half miles downriver, a man driving a large, fiberglass ski boat slowed as he passed. We assumed he was minding his wake. Instead, he shouted across the water, "You better be careful, they're racing the big boats at Johnson's Big Lake." With that he jammed his throttle forward and surged away, leaving us to wallow in his wake.

Forty-five minutes later we found out what he was talking about as the wail and whine of outboards pierced the swamp in waves of disagreeable mechanical sounds that completely disturbed the peaceful float. When we finally got there, Johnson's Big Lake, at 9.65 miles into the paddle, turned out to be a smaller version of Gunter Lake, a few hundred feet shorter, with a similar outline reaching a half mile into the swamp on the Horry side. To make our ride bumpier, the lake entrance served as the turnaround for a dozen or more racing boats. It was a sunny Sunday afternoon and the big boys were definitely out racing. However, it was neither the boats nor the big lake that surprised us most. Rather the 1.5 mile stretch from the lake mouth down to Hughes Landing. This was the widest part of the Little Pee Dee yet, wider and longer than Fork Retch. It was not arrow straight like The Retch, but certainly at least 300 feet wide, plenty of room for ski boats and high speed power boats and on this day a racing hydroplane. The fastest of the pack was the hydroplane which seemed capable of topping 80 miles per hour. The driver spotted all comers a head start, then easily raced past them. Ironically his boat with its superior hull design created the smallest wake. The biggest trouble for us came from the ski boats and high-powered Jon boats which generated unending one to two-foot waves. At one point half a dozen of the boats passed in a drag race and we were forced to turn into the waves to prevent capsizing.

Awaiting the waves generated by racing boats at Hughes Landing below Johnson's Big Lake.

After that we hugged the Horry shore and rocked and rolled down to Hughes Landing, a sandy riverside opening which we thought, after checking the map that morning, would be a good out-of-the-way place to make a stop. However, we found Hughes overrun with cars and trucks and golf carts and a whole lot of people, at least a 100—boaters, swimmers, campers, picnickers and gawkers. Most seemed to be watching the fast boats but a gaggle wandered over to the reedy shoreline where we came ashore. They formed a semicircle around our kayaks.

One young woman in a two-piece bathing suit asked, "Where'd you come from?"

"Fair Bluff in North Carolina," I answered almost truthfully since we had begun there a year earlier.

She pondered my response. "It's a long way," she finally said.

"We really put in today at Locust Tree," Chick said.

"How far is that?" one of the men staring down at us asked.

"Where is it?" another asked.

"About three hours upriver," Chick answered.

"That's a long way," repeated the first young woman we met.

A man walked to the water's edge directly in front and above me. "That's my camper over there," he volunteered. "We are staying on the river. Where'd you come from?"

"Way up the river," someone said from behind the young woman who seemed our most interested interrogator.

"How far to Potato Bed Ferry?" I asked.

The man from the camper wrinkled one side of his face, then the other as if we had demanded he explain $E = mc^2$.

"I don't really know," he said, shaking his head. "I'm not from here."

"Where is that place?" another person asked.

"Potato Bed Ferry is on Highway 378," I said.

"I'll ask about that," the young woman said, still attentive. She walked up the river bank to a group of men working on an outboard motor on the back of one of the racers. They looked like relatives of the rowdy crowd that had squabbled upriver at Dillon County Landing. She returned in a couple of minutes.

"They think you better go back to Locust Tree," she said.

Everyone on the river bank laughed at us, particularly the men gathered around the outboard motor about 20 feet away. We had been typed as some sort of city slickers, or worse yet, foreigners from the still infernal Northern Regions. Yankees who had floated into their domain in girlie kayak thingies. This was probably justice and payback. Certainly I had been guilty of making someone feel an outsider in my youth simply because they didn't come from the same state or county or town. Living overseas most of my life as the outsider ended all that forever. Everyone is a foreigner somewhere and I always try to make strangers feel welcome, knowing the shoe can be on the other foot the next day.

And it was fair for them to think of us as strangers since we regarded them in much the same way. They were interlopers, unknowing strangers to the incredible beauty of a river they could neither hear nor see for the din and the gyrations of the powerboats. We had become eco snobs, not yet full-fledged tree huggers but tending to be among the clan that would ban nearly all the powerboats. We all had probably been born into the same Southern place but only Chick and I could see the natural beauty, I thought. Suddenly my arrogance hit me between the eyes. They were entitled to their definition of beauty and their pursuit of adventure. They had every right to enjoy the good weather, the river, the boats, the speed. But we did not coexist well in the same space.

"How far to Potato Bed Ferry?" I asked another man who had wandered over.

"Oh, it's five or six or seven or eight miles," he answered with a sheepish grin. "It's a long way." He nodded to himself, apparently needing to confirm the wisdom of his imparted knowledge.

We had intended to take a break at Hughes but Chick had had enough. Without a word he pushed back from the reeds and floated into the wake of another power boat, then spun his kayak into the flow of the river and was gone. I followed.

Behind me, the people who had gathered moments earlier fixating on the two strangers, turned as a group to watch a high-powered Jon boat in the channel. It was ploughing in a circle at full throttle with the bow six or seven feet in the air, the transom only inches above the water. The driver, a boy probably about 17 and sporting a toothy smile under a baseball cap worn backward, immediately recognized he was now in the spotlight. He steered his boat into an increasingly tighter circle until it looked like the craft would swivel down backwards in the river and sink. But somehow he stayed afloat, making noise and big waves and even garnering applause from the riverbank.

"Let's get out of here where they can't follow us," Chick called across the water.

I pulled alongside his kayak and we paddled hard for the next bend in the river to break free of our new acquaintances at Hughes Landing. Less than two minutes later the river angled slightly west and we were again floating through cypress and oak forests, passing long stretches of water lily pads and occasional clumps of southern wild rice. The topo maps showed isolated small lakes—Cross, Judy, Hemphill, Cannon, Dill, Riverfield and Burrell Little Lake—on the Marion County side, all of them once parts of old river courses.

Civilization interrupted again ten minutes later on the Marion side as we passed a clear-cut section nearly a mile long. Despite having seen the cutover land bounded by Hemphill Lake and Judy Lake on satellite photos, it was still a surprise to witness the scar on the land since so much of the river forest in the area is now preserved in wildlife management areas.

Half an hour downriver from Hughes we rounded a bend and found a house boat, or more accurately, a floating dock attached to another floating platform with a windowless shed on the deck. The dock was well-made, perhaps 16-feet square, with black plastic floats topped by good timber. The other platform appeared to rest on less reliable Styrofoam floats which we understood are not supposed to be used anymore on the river. Thick yellow ropes at the bow and stern were tied off high in the trees. It did not look like particularly good fishing territory, but was certainly a superior getaway spot.

The river slowly narrowed until it was only about 75 feet across. Angled tree trunks, partially eroded by the powerful flow of the water in flood, reached far out over the channel, putting most of the surface in shadow. It reminded us of a part of the upper river, from Pee Dee State Park down to Allen's Bridge.

At lunch on a sandbar we talked about the powerboats. There had to be a place for such boats, we agreed, but the high powered craft like the hydroplane were overkill. Basically, we would like them to race where we were not. But the discussion was moot. On this summer Sunday, with perfect hot, dry weather from Hughes Landing onward, we were alone on a narrow stretch of the river where the smoke-belching nuisances could never venture. The only other people we saw the rest of the way were a man in a bass boat with his daughter. They waved and he slowed to idle until we were past them. Kindred souls also enjoying the river.

An hour below Hughes we came alongside a point in the river channel less than six hundred feet from Jordan Lake, an old course of the Little Pee Dee in Horry that flanks the present day channel for more than a mile and a half. At high

After Hughes Landing the river narrows, revealing plenty of sandbars for camping or a stopover.

water, we could surely have found a way through the swamp. But not now. We had to be content with the knowledge that from the point parallel with upper Jordan Lake the river runs about a mile due south until it reaches another point parallel to the north end of Old River Lake, another former course, also about 1.5 miles long. Topographical maps show the two lakes were once connected.

We pushed on to Tar Lake, the last body of water opening into the river on the Marion County side before U.S. Highway 378. Finally, half a mile further, a small settlement of houses on the Marion side and the sound of traffic from Highway 378 interrupted the spell of the river. About 15.5 miles downriver, just as the last house slid by on the right, including the Mallard decoys anchored opposite it in the river, the channel narrowed to less than 60-feet and the tree canopy enveloped us in full shadow. Fallen trees, the strainers that are a signature part of the Upper Little Pee Dee, cut into our path again.

The water seemed extremely dark again, the flow brisk because of the narrows. But when I extended my paddle to check the depth I hit sandy bottom less than four feet below. I checked again a minute later in a stretch that seemed even deeper and now there was only three feet of water beneath us. We could hear the trucks and cars now out on Highway 378. Still, the river grew increasingly beautiful, the trees tight around us with each bend offering the opening to a new vista of natural beauty dominated by the great trunks and rich green canopy of the cypresses.

Chick stopped to photograph a new, lush growth of southern wild rice.

A Great Blue Heron, one of the most expert fishers on the Little Pee Dee, lifted off about 100 yards ahead of us. We had been in visual contact for more than a mile on the river and the bird did not seem to understand we too were following the river. It would fly away around the next bend when we came into sight. Inevitably, we would round that bend and startle the great, beautiful bird into flight and out of a good fishing spot in the reeds along the bank.

We passed the wide entrance to Old River Lake on the left and minutes later the steel outline of two bridge construction cranes confronted us above the tree line. They marked the site of the new bridge spanning the river. When we left Chick's car at Potato Bed that morning we identified a floating barge under the bridge as the entry point for the narrow landing channel and it came into view moments later.

We made one last 360 degree turn in the kayaks for final photos before heading to shore. The narrow course of the river was as beautiful as ever behind us as it disappeared into the trees. To the left the broad stretch of water looked like the true course of the river. But it was Old River Lake which ended around a bend in 1,500 feet. Ahead, the river flowed to our right under the massive concrete pilings of the new bridge. Beyond the bridge we could see Byrd Island and the start of the waterway to our next destination, Punch Bowl Landing.

How far is that someone will probably ask us at some point on the next section? Thanks to the people at Hughes Landing, I now have the answer.

It is a long way, I will say. But a beautiful one.

This marker off Highway 378 is reminder of the famous Britton's Neck Ferry used by Francis Marion and of the old settlement between the Little Pee Dee and Great Pee Dee Rivers.

14

Into The Heart Of Francis Marion Country

Potato Bed Ferry to Punch Bowl Landing (8 Miles)

It took us more than a month to get back on the river. Autumn had come to the South Carolina Low Country. The sun glinted off foliage. Flashes of orange mixed with the predominant green along the water. The morning was cool but still shirtsleeve weather, the suffocating humidity only a memory. Mosquitoes had gone wherever they go when they no longer swarm. We had entered that pleasant in-between period after the heat ends and before you must wear a jacket. College football was king again: South Carolina and Clemson fans or Clemson and South Carolina fans, according to loyalties, were now well into their most intense period of hurling infantile insults at each other.

At Potato Bed Ferry the construction barge we had passed on entry to the landing during our last visit was gone. The lifting cranes had moved on, leaving a modern cream white concrete span alive with Highway 378 traffic. At the landing overnight campers had left a stinking, smoldering fire pit roughly ringed by beer cans. Similar debris from perhaps a dozen earlier camp scenes littered the surrounding ground. Something was dead in the underbrush at Potato Bed, perhaps a fish or a possum, and the vultures had not yet found and consumed it. Given the odor and the trash we could not push away from the landing fast enough.

We entered the river at mid-morning. Ahead of us down toward the Great Pee Dee were 14 miles of water designated as a state scenic river section in 1997. We would cover eight miles this day, from Potato Bed to Punch Bowl Landing behind Conway.

From the topographical maps I knew the appearance of this stretch of water and the wetlands would be essentially the same as 230 years earlier when Francis Marion and his scouts galloped through the region. Paddling the river had rekindled my already considerable interest in Marion and I had come upon mention of Potato Ferry the previous night while rereading Professor Robert D. Bass' book *Swamp Fox*.[32] That crossing is on the Black River, but nevertheless called up images of Marion's bedraggled partisans. They were sometimes only 30 or 40 in number, bedrolls strapped to their lathered horses and a musket or rifle in hand. They almost always rode to the river in haste, rushing toward an engagement or even more likely, in wild flight, successfully eluding British regulars and loyalist militia who decried the savage, uncivilized colonists unwilling to come out and fight and die European style on an open field in neat rows and columns.

Tres Hyman, a Revolutionary War expert from Cartersville in Florence County, said he has heard more than once that Potato Bed and Potato Ferry got their names from the potatoes that farmers planted near the landing. "They went well with fish cooked on the riverbank." he said. "No way to know if that could be true but it makes a good story."[33]

The river splits just below the Highway 378 Bridge. Chick took the channel on the west side of Byrd Island while I stayed left and moved alongside Pitts Landing which looked a far better place to launch from than Potato Bed. An open expanse of lush grass that grew down to the water's edge was more inviting than anything upriver at Potato Bed. On this morning, campers moved around outside their tent and van.

"Good place to stay," a man folding a sleeping bag answered when I inquired about their night. "You can camp at any of the landings," he said. "That's really a nice thing about South Carolina."

Their campsite was clean. Four folding chairs were arranged neatly around a fire pit. There was no trash or beer cans lying around and all four campers looked well prepared for the outdoors. Their late model van had a camper top. They wore Bermudas, t-shirts and woolen toboggans and appeared to be college students. They easily passed my inspection as responsible campers.

Pitts Landing below Potato Bed Ferry is a popular camping spot on the river.

"Have a good one," I said and pulled back into the current.

I was the last to arrive at the south end of Byrd Island, a mile downriver. Chick was waiting for me with a map in hand. I had stopped to photograph the light and shadow of a grouping of what I thought were needle palm plants bathed in the morning sunlight on the east bank. I counted more than a dozen plants spread out in fans each four to five feet wide. When I began our river trips I probably would not have paused to check out the growth. But Chick's awareness of plant life had sharpened my interest and now I could not learn enough. When he saw the digital camera images he corrected me. *Rhapidophyllum hystrix*, needle palm, did grow in South Carolina, he said, but the northernmost range was Colleton and Jasper Counties, nearer to the Georgia state line. I had photographed *Sabal minor*, dwarf palmetto, which he noted was rarer in blackwater swamps than in red water or brown water swamps like the Great Pee Dee.

We found a houseboat anchored in a cove a few hundred feet beyond the end of Byrd Island. The simple tin structure atop a floating platform was perhaps eight by twelve and was anchored alongside a floating dock. A spit of grass-covered mud protected the craft from the current. We rounded the next bend and saw a snake crossing the river. It swam with its head several inches above the water and seemed to double its speed as it sighted us. Chick was farther to the right and about to intercept the snake when it stopped in midstream, lowered its head and formed an imperfect circle with its body. The oblong form drifted downstream much like a round piece of vine in the river. But we could see its eyes on our craft.

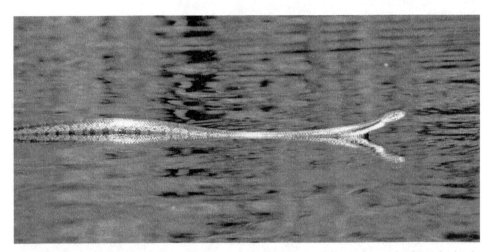

A Banded Water Snake gives up on playing dead in the river and heads for reeds along the bank above Punch Bowl Landing.

This continued for about a minute as we floated within 20 feet. When it was obvious we were not fooled, the snake quickly came back to life and headed for the bank in powerful S-shaped undulations that propelled it quickly across the water. Afterwards, examination of the photographs revealed we had probably seen another Northern or Banded Water Snake, similar to the one we photographed at Locust Tree Court trying to swallow a large catfish whole.

In the next bend Chick stopped under a tupelo tree to point out the dark purple fruit hanging from the branches. The so-called swamp olive is the fruit of *Nyssa aquatica*, the water tupelo. The fruit, dotted with pale spots, is a favorite of wildlife. Wood ducks and other birds, squirrels, raccoons and deer all feast regularly on the fruit.[34]

Our goal this day was Punch Bowl Landing eight miles downriver and southwest of Conway. Along the way, on the Marion County side, from a mile or so downriver to the junction with the Great Pee Dee, we would be alongside the South Carolina Department of Natural Resources Wildlife Management Agency's 25,688 acre Woodbury Tract. We were, in essence, passing the neck of Britton's Neck, the crucible of General Marion's adventures with the British. Several historic sites, including the Britton's Neck ferry launch, are within the boundaries of the tract.

I recalled another day of exploration in the Neck with Bob Barrett[35], the former head of the Francis Marion Trail Commission and timber consultant and Francis

Marion expert Tres Hyman. We met at a store Barrett called 'The Park and Blow' at the intersection of S.C. Highway 908 and U.S. 378 at the entrance to the Woodbury tract. From there across 378 it is only a ten-minute drive down Dunham's Bluff Road to the Great Pee Dee. And directly across the river lies Snow Island, where Marion hid from the British on many occasions. On the downriver side of the Marion County landing Hyman pointed out a six-foot-high ridge just inside the tree line. It was the still visible outline of a redoubt built by Marion and his men more than 230 years earlier.

Five minutes' drive up Highway 378 we turned off onto a dirt road that took us into a timber tract along the river. "This was a Colonial road on which Marion and the British traveled," Hyman said. A few hundred yards further we pulled into an opening near the river. Barrett and I followed Hyman a few hundred feet to a point alongside an arm of the river where the craft for Port's Ferry docked.

Francis Marion experts Tres Hyman (l) and Bob Barrett study Revolutionary War locator maps at Dunham's Bluff Landing opposite Snow Island on the Great Pee Dee River.

Here Marion had crossed to engage in the Battle of Black Mingo. Volunteers had joined him there for engagements and both British and American troops had crossed the little strip of land and the river beyond both ways nearly 233 years earlier. "It doesn't look that impressive now, but it has great historical significance," Hyman said.

Later Hyman, Barrett and I retraced our route and drove down the Woodbury tract road to the turnoff for the abandoned home site of Marion biographer Robert

Bass. All that remains of the place where Bass and his family moved in the early 20th century are two massive live oaks, one of them fallen, and scattered bricks from the house foundation.

A short distance further down the Woodbury Road, at a pile of slag used for fill, a side road on the right continues for several miles into the swamp. There it forks again and from that point we walked the road toward the Britton's Ferry site. In about 30 minutes we reached the Great Pee Dee but were unable to get to the actual ferry crossing because of high water. The single lane road followed the same track used by Marion's mounted troops and the British regulars.

The Woodbury Wildlife Management Area and Heritage Preserve is one of the state's greatest natural and historical treasures. It is open to everyone free of charge and encompasses a bottomland forest with 11.5 miles of frontage on the Little Pee Dee and 27.5 miles of frontage on the Great Pee Dee. The tract was acquired by the state from International Paper in a cooperative agreement in which the Nature Conservancy and The Conservation Fund assisted with the purchase on behalf of South Carolina.

The South Carolina Department of Natural Resources says the habitats found at Woodbury "include over a dozen Carolina Bays, a long sandy ridge supporting longleaf pine and loblolly pine forests, and other isolated wetlands. The forested wetland is home to the Kentucky Warbler, Louisiana Waterthrush, Rusty blackbird, the Swallow-tailed Kike and the Swainson's Warbler."[36]

Back on the river with a thousand ibises

In the first hour down from Potato Bed Ferry Chick and I saw a few ibises fishing in the water alongside the sandbars. And then they began flying in front of us in increasingly larger groups. Soon there were twenty or more at a time cruising the river from above before alighting in the high branches of cypress trees along the banks.

During the first three hours we probably saw at least a thousand of these birds. The ibises, Chick explained, were the White Ibis, *Eudocimus albus*, with classic white plumage and a reddish-yellow decurved bill. They flew with long necks extended and spindly legs trailing. They constantly took off and alighted in new trees, always downriver. We heard bird squeals and nearly unceasing honking as they communicated. Although some of the ibis migrate, Chick said, most remain on the river year round. We never were far from at least several dozen of the birds for the entire eight miles of the paddle.

This Little Pee Dee section is flanked by another succession of lakes—Phillips, Page, Sandy Island, Richard, James, Sampson—all of them, as we had seen along the lower river, parts of old courses now cut off from the main channel.

We paddled slowly, agreeing quickly that of all the memorable sections on the wide river below Fork Retch, this was the most beautiful thus far. The water was open, so broad that even the largest fallen trees did not hamper passage. Spanish

White Ibis began to appear all along the route down from Locust Tree Landing to Punch Bowl.

moss hung from hundreds of trees, wafting gray veils that filtered the sunlight and the clean-smelling autumn breeze. The thermometer nudged 74 and stayed there. We saw no clear-cuts in the first three hours and finally concluded there would be none. The river experience here would be unspoiled—wide water, abundant wildlife, natural forest.

In that third hour we did see something extraordinary—people. Three of them in a small fishing boat powered by a five horsepower Johnson motor. We caught sight of their boat as it moved slowly along the Marion County side when we rounded a bend. They slowed even more as we exchanged greetings. They were a family—man, woman and daughter—enjoying the fall foliage along the river. We floated alongside them for about a minute and then they headed downriver under power but at a pace not much quicker than ours.

It was a good day for talk and we hit the highlights. The Obama-Romney presidential campaign, travel to the West Indies, tennis, our family, our family some more, aches and pains and finally general agreement that it would be a rare individual who could be having more pleasure than the two of us now riding the river.

A small houseboat occupies a secluded section of a cove below Potato Bed Ferry Landing.

We passed the entrance to Sampson Lake. If you have to get off the river, you can do so here, although you must follow an old course of the river on a winding one-half-mile paddle to an interior landing on a second lake we think is also called Sampson. The landing is connected by a dirt track to the main Woodbury Tract dirt road.

Another mile downriver we turned up a slough on the Marion County side and paddled 500 feet into the swamp. We were looking for another landing and another way out of the swamp, if needed. The satellite photo showed a house and an open field at the end of McLeod Road on the Woodbury Tract. When we got to the end of the slough we were greeted by "No Trespassing" signs.

In the distance we could see a large cabin with several outbuildings spread around a manicured grass lawn. Chick thought it was the property of the Department of Natural Resources, but the warning signs stopped us from investigating too closely. It is worth knowing where it is on the river, two thirds of the way to Punch Bowl, since it looks to be a second exit from the river on the west side.

A few minutes later reentering the river we saw more people. Two men in a bass boat passed, moving slowly—no fishing poles in sight, just sightseeing. That made five people for the day, about one person per river mile. Two miles further downriver we crossed under a double row of high voltage power lines. The cross pieces of the towering creosote poles provided the best perch in the area for vultures and there were at least three dozen of them looking down at us. Every few seconds one of the birds would find an open spot and spread its wings in the wind, drying its feathers.

Just under the power lines the old flow of the Little Pee Dee branches off down Russ Creek into the lake of the same name. From there the course parallels the Little Pee Dee before it joins up a half mile from the junction with the big river. This route is popular because it flows past the Tree House, a Little Pee Dee landmark. It continues on for five and a half miles through Russ Lake before swinging east to rejoin the river a half mile before the junction.

This day we took the main channel of the river and minutes later rounded a bend to see a large houseboat with a floating dock tied to the trees in a cove within sight of the power lines. It was the best preserved of the houseboats we had encountered but far too close to the high voltage power lines for comfort.

Fifteen minutes downriver, off a sandy bank on the Horry side, three children and a man were swimming in the river as we passed. Punch Bowl Landing was visible in the distance on the Horry side. It would be our last stop before reaching the end of our journey, the junction of the two rivers.

The final section of the Little Pee Dee before the junction is marked by a series of houseboats anchored to the Horry County shore.

Cypress forests flank both sides of the river leading to the junction.

15

To The Great Pee Dee Junction

Punch Bowl Landing to the Tanyard Landing on the Great Pee Dee (5 Miles)
And Russ Creek alternate to the Tanyard (8.5 Miles)

We could not have selected better weather for the final section of the Little Pee Dee. Although it was November, the sun was brilliant, the sky blue and the temperature predicted to reach the mid-seventies by early afternoon. The good weather made me want to phone my friend Albert Finocchiaro in Syracuse, N.Y., and listen to his description of the snow there. But it would have been bad form to talk about our fine day when I knew he was up to his shins in snow. I would call later, perhaps when we had our own little sprinkling of snow in the swamp. Our trip would take us five miles and we knew the scenery would be a continuation of the outstanding paddle we had experienced down from Potato Bed Ferry.

Punch Bowl is an easy put-in with parking everywhere and ample space for camping. A wide, paved county boat ramp and a floating dock accommodate all sizes of river craft. When we drove up to the landing we were the third vehicle there. A man with a South Carolina veterans license tag on his truck was behind the steering wheel reading the morning paper. He gave us a glance over the top of his eyeglasses, then went back to his newspaper. A few yards upstream, along the river bank, two campers emerged from a tent, shielded their eyes from the sun with outstretched hands and walked briskly toward the woods—there are no facilities at the landing.

We paddled easily down the wide channel until we reached a point about 1.3 miles below Punch Bowl. There we entered a narrow, shallow slough reaching 500 feet back into the swamp on the Horry County side. We paddled into an oblong-shaped lake Chick had spotted on an aerial map. The deep green appearance of the water surface had caught his eye. Once we entered the lake we found the color resulted from a disappointing combination of slime, dirty alligator weed, duckweed and river debris, including numerous green plastic bottles, soda cans and the other assorted detritus that had come down river over the years. From several thousand feet overhead, it had appeared beautiful. Up close, it was a mostly filthy covering. Chick was determined to photograph the center of the lake and pushed on through the weeds. He made it about 200 feet before the vegetation stopped him. He took a few pictures and backtracked.

Back on the river we heard an outboard and watched as an aluminum Jon boat powered by a big Mercury outboard skidded at speed around the bend below us. A woman lounged in the front taking the sun, a man in a baseball cap drove and another woman sat beside him talking on a cell phone. In front of them, in the middle of the boat, a portable generator filled the rest of the open space.

We assumed they were coming back from one of the houseboats anchored downriver. The boat didn't slow going past and afterwards we dealt with a series of good-sized waves before things were calm again. A mile further we passed two fishermen putting in at a sandy landing beside a houseboat. In the next two hours we passed perhaps a dozen houseboats. Unbroken great cypress forests flanked the river and we seldom saw dry land, save a couple of places to put in a boat. We also saw no clear cuts anywhere on the route. Here the river belt stretches to more than a mile and a half wide and this is the one section, above all, where you definitely do not want to be stranded.

From the air the roofs of the houseboats catch your eye, resembling shiny white rectangles, nearly all of them along the east bank. Up close, we could see the houseboats were elaborate, well-built floating structures, anchored by steel cables, and equipped with all kinds of amenities including electricity, running water and satellite TV.

Someone had taken the time, effort and risk to nail more signs high up on several cypress trees along the east side. Script letters burnished into one plank, told us "He's All I Need!" Another sign, professionally done, advised, "Thou Shalt Not Commit Adultery" and directed us to the Prayer Center and the A.T.C.

Christian School. The Prayer Center and School also reminded us at another point downriver "Thou Shalt Not Covet Thy Neighbor's Goods." A little further, a distinctly secular sign pointed us toward "Bunny's" and gave a Mullins phone number. It reminded me of a high school friend, Bunny Beeson, who founded Wildlife Action, a well-respected conservation group that owns and manages 50,000 acres of land.[37]

The once verdant swamp foliage had changed completely in recent weeks. The hardwoods were nearly bare of leaves, revealing a backdrop of blue sky where opaque waves of green had once moved in unison with the wind. The bald cypresses caught the eye like pale masts topped by canopies shedding their needle leaves and dangling long shawls of thick Spanish moss. The grass along the river remained a constant, still brilliant green while floating leaves of every shape and fall hue accompanied us downriver.

We were coming into that short local season, beginning in November and lasting until sometime in February or early March, when locals lament what they

The Russ Creek route is distinguished by the massive cypress trees along the waterway.

call cold weather. All the while the temperatures start mostly in the forties at daybreak, reaching the sixties under afternoon blue skies and brilliant sunshine. A dustup of snow and some ice on the roads might interrupt the fair weather and the mercury could possibly fall into the teens or twenties a time or two before warm weather returns. These same locals, among them some friends and relatives, would bemoan the discomfort caused by being forced to wear a light coat over short sleeves or maybe even a winter jacket and insulated boots for a couple of days. At the same time, half a million people, most of them migrated from the northern half of the country to sunny spots along the Carolina coast, would revel in the same weather, laughing at the brief cold period, thinking it near tropical compared to what they had known before moving to the South.

The Tree House Route

The alternative to our direct route downriver from Punch Bowl to the Tanyard Landing is the most unique section of the river along its entire 109-mile course. The Russ Creek route runs eight miles through swamps on the west side of the main channel, and we returned to paddle it almost a year after going down the main river in November of 2012.

It was September 21, the last day of summer. The river was already filled with floating leaves and on this Saturday anglers were out everywhere after being thwarted by high water for much of July and August. There had been at least 50 trucks with boat trailers at Punch Bowl when we put in. And as we learned quickly on the river, more than a few of the crowd were anxious to run at full throttle despite low water, oblivious to the problems they were causing those trying to fish the promising spots beside lily pads and in the lee of sandbars.

At the one-mile mark upriver we entered an arm mistakenly thinking we were headed for the cut that would take us into Russ Creek and the alternate route. We did so because we knew the cut was under the high voltage power lines where we remembered seeing vultures drying their wings the previous November. But the trip turned out to be a short one into a dead arm of the river. We found only a backwater in the swamp filled with ibises and a couple of Great Blue Herons and photographed them as they gawked at the intruders without leaving their perches.

Back on the river we paddled another one-third of a mile upriver where we came to a power line crossing again, the right one this time. The partially hidden exit, which is just over a mile upriver from Punch Bowl, is on the Marion County side and only about 15 feet wide. But even at low water there was still a good flow into the diversion. We entered the slow-moving stream that meanders between massive cypresses with bases up to 16 feet wide. High water marks on the trees showed the flood stage level in early summer had been eight feet above us.

If the massive trees had not been so inaccessible, they would probably have been logged years earlier, Chick called out to me over his shoulder as he paddled a few feet ahead. A few seconds later he shouted for me to join him on the backside of one of the big cypresses. I found him pointing toward the limbs of a water tupelo.

A Green-Fly orchid found on a tree branch on Russ Creek was the first reported sighting of this epiphytic orchid in Marion County.

"That is a Green-fly orchid, *Epidendrum canopseum!*" he declared with a note of triumph in his voice. "I think it might be the first recorded in the area. It's near the northern limit of its growing range." This epiphytic orchid grows as far up the coast as North Carolina, he said, and thrives on the humid, moist conditions present deep in the swamp along Russ Creek. We snapped away with our cameras at a frilly collection of dark green petal-like leaves that seemed to turn a reddish purple where the light hit the plant. Chick later confirmed by checking plant distribution records that it was the first sighting in Marion County. Epiphytic orchids grow non-parasitically on trees, he said, taking nutrients and moisture from the air and the surface of the tree host.

The first part of the Russ Creek route is narrow, winding through the swamp before opening twice, at 1.5 miles and 1.7 miles, into slough-like channels. After that, there is another half mile of narrow water. This route is sometimes called the Tree House Paddle because it goes past a tree house that has become part of Little Pee Dee lore. The two-story structure is visible on aerial photos as a white reflection in the cypress canopy at the 2.5 mile mark of the paddle. C.P. said his late cousin Gary Mincey, a former game warden, was once stranded on the river when his boat motor failed. He survived a cold night by climbing into the treehouse and wrapping himself in a rug until help came the next day.

Looking up from water level, the whole structure appeared in danger of collapse. The Tree House is nailed to and built around cypress trunks in a crazy quilt design that includes an aluminum Jon boat that is part of a porch wall. A fire barrel with a rickety metal chimney hangs over one side. There is a sizeable interior room, where Cousin Gary probably slept, and a second story penthouse of sorts. There is no dry land even in low water. You have to climb steps coming out of the swamp water to get aboard. Some of the walls are rusting tin sheets and the second story room walls are fabricated from particle board guaranteed to eventually disintegrate in the humid swamp. A partially collapsed ramp connected to a platform out back might have once been the walkway to an overhead toilet. The celebrated Tree House is not that much to look at, but one of those places most visitors want to see. It meets the requirements of my Balkan friend Marco Dulic's three-time rule. First time, last time, only time, he says about any less than memorable experience.

The Tree House is a revered and battered two-story structure in the swamp along the Russ Creek route.

A few hundred yards further we worked our way through a maze of cypresses and came upon the secluded fishing spot of Michelle Jones and her husband Peanut. The Lake City couple was seated in comfortable-looking arm chairs mounted on a wide-bottomed bass boat. Peanut used a fly rod with a plastic bobber on the line and crickets as bait. Michelle was casting with a spinning reel. Peanut Jones, who is white-haired and looks to be in his fifties, said his brother gave him his nickname when he was a tiny infant first home from the hospital and reputedly no larger than a peanut. While we were talking he caught a hand-sized panfish and threw it into an ice chest behind him. Michelle caught an even bigger fish moments later. I asked if the fish were Morgans, the name my father had taught me.

"We call them Warmouths," Peanut said, but acknowledged they might be known locally as Morgans.

Lepomis gulosus, Chick confirmed, are sometimes called Morgans in the Low Country. They are dark, have dirty brown stripes and a bright orange spot

Michelle Jones of Lake City pulls in a Morgan on Russ Creek in front of her husband Peanut.

A soft shell turtle keeps a close eye on boaters nearing a log perch on the Russ Creek route.

near the base of the dorsal fin and can grow to be a foot-long and weigh two pounds, he added.

The Joneses had put in at a landing on the Woodbury tract, not far from the power line after driving an hour from Lake City. "We'd like to find a house to buy on the river down here, but there aren't that many of them where we want to be," Peanut said.

The open water gradually widened as we continued downstream. Soon we were in a slow-moving channel about 100 feet across and that continued for the next couple of miles. The trees were alive with birds, primarily ibises and herons. We were entertained by the antics of an Anhinga, or snakebird, a long-necked bird that swam in front of our kayaks. It twirled in the water, then submerged, hunting for fish to spear with its sharp bill. It emerged several times ahead of us and gulped down its catch, then

A young wading bird remains still as paddlers approach on Russ Creek

headed out on the hunt again, its long neck and head high out of the water until it suddenly went under.

We were watching *Anhinga anhinga,* Chick said. The bird reminded him of the famed great cormorants in Japan and China. They are trained to catch fish under the water but are stopped from swallowing prey, usually by a constrictive ring around their lower necks. Their trainers take the fish and send the birds back down in the water again. Our Anhinga was sharing nothing, however, flicking its head in the air and pulsing its neck to down whatever it speared under the water.

At 4.8 miles into the paddle, the second of the three routes downriver from Punch Bowl came in on the left. A look at the map shows this channel is entered 1.5 miles downriver from Punch Bowl on the west side of the main river.

There was no dry land in sight so we lunched in our kayaks. While we ate with our craft lodged between cypress knees, we watched a light breeze blow the leaves on the water surface upstream. It was not a good omen and as we descended toward Russ Lake the wind stiffened. At this point we were 5.3 miles into the paddle from Punch Bowl and could have returned to the main river by following the channel to the left for a third of a mile.

We followed Russ Lake, a half-mile long body of water over 700-feet wide at the opening, and battled a brisk headwind until reaching the sheltered south shore. There we made a hard left into the channel arm leading back to the main river. We were now seven miles into the paddle. In Russ Lake and down to the junction we saw evidence of tidal fluctuation on the Little Pee Dee. The tidal bore, which pushes more than 33 miles up the Great Pee Dee, was not as obvious on the Little Pee Dee. But it was there. A wet ring around the cypress trees showed the water level had been higher hours earlier. In Russ Lake the black water of the Little Pee Dee became increasingly brown as we descended, revealing the backflow from the Great Pee Dee.

This area of the river is best understood by viewing aerial photos. The overhead view shows the complexity of the wetlands with water descending in three, then two distinctive vein like channels. Finally the two channels join a few hundred yards upriver from the junction with the Great Pee Dee.

From the junction, which is five miles direct from Punch Bowl and about eight miles via Russ Creek, the dark waters of the Little Pee Dee and the muddy flow of the Great Pee Dee continue for almost a mile as separate, thick ribbons, one dark, one muddy, before the big river finally dominates the flow.

A kayaker starts up the Great Pee Dee after rounding the bend from the Little Pee Dee (right). Photo L.L. Gaddy

On our first trip to the junction in November 2012, we turned upstream at the sandbar delta covering the Y where the rivers meet. Despite a lack of wind we immediately felt strong resistance to our progress, more we thought than the normal power of the downstream current. There was a light chop on the water, which we at first failed to recognize as a sign of the tidal bore pushing up from the coast. The wet mud along the bank was at least two feet above the water line; the river had been higher only a few hours earlier. The chop and the Great Pee Dee current against us made the last eight-tenths of a mile to the Tanyard Landing a good workout to complete the day. The sun was setting and the day suddenly cool, the temperature probably in the low fifties as we waded ashore.

We came out of the river at a campsite where a man fished while warming his backside with the dancing flames of a wood fire. The camper was Brian Carbino of Myrtle Beach, a transplanted New Yorker with a lifelong love of the outdoors. He said he came down to South Carolina to avoid the harsh winters in New York. He was grilling pork chops and awaiting the arrival of his wife and mother-in-law by car. He had put up a small tent and planned to spend the night on the river after they left. We accepted his invitation to warm up at the fire.

Carbino said he knew the Adirondack Mountains of upstate New York well, but now preferred to spend his free time along the South Carolina rivers in his area.

Brian Carbino of Myrtle Beach enjoys camping and fishing along South Carolina rivers.

I called him a few days later and he said the meal had gone well. Unfortunately, he had been bitten by a spider on his eyelid during the night and the swelling had been uncomfortable. But he would continue camping, he said.

Earlier, when we were securing Chick's car for later pickup at the Tanyard, we met two mule riders on a morning trip along the sandy roads of the 26,000-acre Woodbury Tract. They had come down from Pamplico in Florence County with their mounts in trailers and were spending the day in the saddle. It is a good place to ride, they told us. You would have to say that Gen. Francis Marion also judged the area between the two Pee Dee rivers a fine place to ride. And finer still to hide.

Mule riders from Pamplico, S.C., take a break from a ride on the Woodbury Tract on Britton's Neck. Photo L.L. Gaddy

At dusk we lashed the kayaks to Chick's car and headed up the bumpy 14-mile Woodbury dirt road to Highway 378. We were both unusually quiet. There had been no champagne or celebration or high fives. Just an unspoken feeling of accomplishment after paddling the final section of the Little Pee Dee, a journey from Red Bluff Lake to the Great Pee Dee junction.

A marker on the Lumber River shows the way back to Fair Bluff, a Columbus County town just across the North Carolina line.

The Lumber River flows behind the Columbus County, N.C., town of Fair Bluff.

16

Keeping A Promise On The Lumber River

Fair Bluff, N.C., to Fork Retch, S.C. (20 Miles)

The first river trip we took for this book was not on the Little Pee Dee but on the Lumber River, the primary tributary of the Little Pee Dee. It was a brief journey, only 20 miles, done in two sections, from Fair Bluff, N.C., to Nichols, S.C., and then on to Fork Retch where the Lumber joins the Little Pee Dee. Paddling these two sections was a tribute to my cousin Ben Brown, a great outdoorsman and brave man who survived combat in Vietnam as a decorated Green Beret but could not overcome cancer.

Chick and I met on a sunny but decidedly cool March day in 2011 at the N.C. Highway 904 Bridge in downtown Fair Bluff on the Lumber. Our first destination,

Nichols Bridge, was 16 miles downriver just inside the South Carolina line. From there it was four miles farther to the junction with the Little Pee Dee.

A few months earlier I planned to make the trip to Nichols Bridge with Ben. He and I, and another cousin, Gene Connelly, had experienced about every outdoor adventure young boys could think of along the two rivers by the time we finished high school in 1963. In late 2010, Ben wanted to paddle his favorite river, the Lumber, to signal his recovery from throat and mouth cancer surgery and a rigorous radiation treatment program the previous autumn.

But his condition worsened over the winter and two weeks earlier, after a valiant battle, he died. I promised him two days before his death that I would make the trip for him and for Gene, who had passed away the previous summer, also of cancer. That's how Chick and I ended up in Fair Bluff, a sleepy, little Columbus County river town, split on the east by the railroad line to Nichols and flanked uncomfortably close on the west by the river. The outside air temperature was probably sixty but the water decidedly colder as we walked up to our knees in the river in sand shoes, straddled our kayaks and settled in. I first pulled on dry wool socks and my favorite brogans. With luck I'd be able to dismount at stops along the way without getting my toes wet again. Chick simply slipped out of his sandals, propped his feet up to dry and let the gentle late winter sun bathe his face and warm his toes as we crossed under the 904 bridge.

The quarter-mile stretch of the Lumber after the bridge in Fair Bluff is scenic but quite dangerous. At low water great lengths of exposed sandbar and adjacent shallows beckon those who want to wade. But even then there are holes just off the end of the sandy stretches and beneath the overhanging limbs draped with Spanish moss. A few years earlier five people drowned in the river within sight of the bridge, and those were not the first swimming deaths there. The Lumber was known in colonial times as Drowning Creek and nearly every settlement and boat landing hereabouts has its sad tale of someone who perished in the dark waters. The name of the river was changed by the North Carolina legislature from Drowning Creek to the Lumber River in 1809, recognizing the importance of the logging industry and also providing a more acceptable name for a main waterway in Eastern North Carolina. The Lumbee Indian Tribe, based in Robeson County, wants the river called the Lumbee, a tribal name it adopted in the 1950s.

At the point we entered the Lumber it had already passed through four North Carolina counties from its headwaters in Scotland County, N.C. From there it flows over 130 miles through Hoke, Robeson and into Columbus County before entering South Carolina. The river joins the Little Pee Dee at Fork Retch between Nichols and Mullins. The Lumber is the only blackwater river to be designated a National Wild and Scenic River by the U.S. Department of the Interior and has its own state park. The lower part of the river has been designated a North Carolina State Canoe Trail.

Lumber River State Park follows the course of the river between Orrum, N.C., and Fair Bluff and covers an area of about 9,000 acres. Native plant and animal life along the river are protected within the park while scenic camping and nature study points are provided at the site of a former settlement called Princess Anne. The main entrance to the park is on Princess Road, which runs from Highway 904 outside Fair Bluff. The Lumber often floods, particularly in winter, periodically rising to the back doors of Main Street businesses in Fair Bluff. One of those back doors belonged for half a century to my friend P.L. Elvington, Jr., who ran a pharmacy with one of the last remaining custom made marble top soda fountains in the Carolinas. The counter, mirrors and soda and ice cream fixtures dated to the early part of the 20th century, and P.L. delighted in serving up an authentic ice cream float from behind the counter. The counter and pharmacy are still there but P.L. now spends his time hunting, fishing and visiting friends.

The South Carolina line is less than an hour downstream from the 904 Bridge and is marked by a white stake and also a weather-beaten concrete pillar along the east bank. In addition, a metal road sign nailed to one of the cypresses indicates Fair Bluff is three miles upstream. Horry County is on the left and Dillon County on the right as you enter South Carolina. A few miles further Dillon County gives way to Marion County on the right, or west side.

We paused again a few minutes later in mid-river. The red maples were already in bloom and Chick maneuvered his kayak to get a good photograph. A Wood Duck launched into a noisy takeoff as we rounded the next bend.

Four and one-half miles downriver, we paddled level with Griffin's Landing, a settlement of perhaps a dozen buildings set on a sandy ridge on the Horry side. Architecture along the Lumber, like the Little Pee Dee, ranges from forlorn, tin-topped shacks and rusting house trailers to split level brick homes with manicured lawns. Sometimes the worst is adjacent to the best. The houses closest to the river, unless built on a bluff, tend to be constructed well above the high water level on pilings.

Access to this section of the Lumber is from Causey Road, which reaches from Fair Bluff nearly two-thirds of the way to Nichols. Causey begins as a paved road in Fair Bluff, turns to sand at the South Carolina line and continues parallel to the railroad until it turns to cross the tracks near the old sand plant upriver from the Nichols railroad trestle.

On the eighth bend down from Griffins Landing, at 6.5 miles, we saw two more small homes set back in the trees. Later we found them on the map and determined that Constitution Dr., a narrow dirt track, comes into the sandy ridge from a turnoff on Griffins Landing Road. A little over a mile further we passed a canal dug on the east side of the river and headed up it for a short distance until stopped by backwash debris from the river. Satellite images show the canal runs another 1,000 feet to a clearing with a tin-roofed structure.

On this trip we rounded each bend hoping for signs of Amis Mill, a Revolutionary War encampment where Francis Marion and a small number of his men had hidden from the British in 1780 following the Battle of Black Mingo Creek. They were under the protection of Capt. Thomas Amis, a leader of the revolution in North Carolina. Black Mingo was one of half a dozen skirmishes fought by Marion's men in the last five months of 1780. The guerrilla attacks came at a time when colonial fortunes were sagging. The British sought to break the rebellion by quelling the uprising in the Southern colonies. The first step was the capture of Charleston in May 1780.

Marion and a small force, sometimes no more than a dozen men, other times more than a hundred, harassed the British in the lower half of the state, and especially in the Pee Dee. In a series of skirmishes using hit and run tactics Marion fought the British regulars at Great Savannah (August 20), Blue Savannah (September 4), Black Mingo (September 29), Tearcoat Swamp (October 26), Georgetown (November 15) and Halfway Swamp (December 12-13). Black Mingo is located off present-day Highway 41 between Johnsonville and Andrews just below the junction of 41 with S.C. Highway 513. My father always called Highway 41 'the road without pity' because of the remoteness along long sections of the highway. A marker near the Black Mingo site records the battle as having occurred on Sept. 14 but Sept. 29 is accepted as the correct date by most historians.

Mary Alice Thompson, who heads the historical society in Fair Bluff, stands before the Revolutionary War site of Amis Mill.

We had a purported latitude-longitude reading for the Amis Mill site, but when we reached that point on the river below Griffins Landing the locater proved inaccurate. The site of the mill, I was to learn nearly a month later, was not below Fair Bluff and not on the present-day run of the river, but above it and nearly two miles inland from the current river channel. I drove there one spring day with Bob Barrett, then head of the Francis Marion Trail Commission and Mary Alice Thompson, head of the historical society in Fair Bluff. The mill remains are on private land along a narrow dirt causeway that crosses a cypress swamp outside Fair Bluff. The causeway ends where the swamp flow crosses the foundation remains of the mill sluice. The road resumes on the other side of the sluice. Satellite photos show the faint trace of the old causeway road emerging into a ploughed field beyond the swamp. The Amis Mill remains are below the foundation of a mill house constructed in the 19th century. The swamp to the east of the causeway appears unchanged from Marion's time, the shadowy beauty of cypress trees rising from algae-decked dark water far more authentic that any of the swamp scenes in the 2000 film *The Patriot* with Mel Gibson. While the film did not feature Marion, or other South Carolina revolutionary war luminaries like Andrew Pickens, the Wizard Owl, and Thomas Sumter, the Gamecock, the exploits are certainly theirs, overdressed and inaccurately recorded with typical Hollywood bombast.

On this day Chick and I were unaware of the true Amis Mill site and didn't give up hope of finding it until we paddled on into the next long bend past Griffin's Landing where there is another Drowning Creek reminder, a white cross placed on a promontory on the west bank at a point where a dirt road comes down to the river. It looked like a place where children might swim and the water would have cut deep holes at the outside turn of the bend, not far from the cross.

Cora's Landing settlement is a mile downriver from the cross, 10.5 miles below Fair Bluff. Here the Lumber has shifted course twice in the last half century, forming twin oxbows. We took the second cut-through and passed trailer houses, a battered wood frame shack and other structures before paddling alongside another canal cut from the river bank into the swamp, reaching back almost 250 feet from the main channel.

Our first stop was a fine white sandbar on the east side of the second bend below Cora's Landing. It was nearly at the same spot I had camped on an autumn night almost fifty years earlier with my cousins Ben and Gene. I had flown this section of river with Ben in the summer of 2009 after our cousin Gene's death. Ben was still getting over mouth cancer treatment himself, but he told me he wanted to fly the river for old time's sake. The next day we lifted off from Marion. Visibility was 25 miles as we climbed to a thousand feet and picked up the highway leading into Nichols. Above the grain storage plant outside town we recalled a Christmas hunt in the swamps. He and I got caught in the middle of a sleet storm at Widow's Lake on the river and had to start a fire to dry our clothes before walking home. The only dry fire starter material available was three one-dollar bills and the paper labels from some canned pork and beans. Somehow we coaxed a flame from the bits of paper with a magnesium spark and added pieces of fat lighter chopped from a downed pine on the sandhill. When we had a roaring fire under a lean-two of wet pine boughs and were warm, we just talked. We were 12. A lifetime later, our best times were still spent just talking.

Ben Brown, a decorated Green Beret combat veteran, was a superb outdoorsman. The Lumber and Little Pee Dee were his favorite rivers.

On our flight in 2009 we joined the Lumber River outside Nichols and flew the winding route to Fair Bluff and on up to U.S. Highway 74 near Boardman, N.C. There, I pointed the nose west towards Marion and told Ben "Fly us back, Bud." He didn't hesitate to take the yoke and flew confidently without nerves. Flying in an airplane had always been calming for him, he said. I believe his focusing on the river and the swamps we had known for half a century helped him shut out the cancer for a short time and recall other days in the back of a Huey helicopter starting a mission with his team. Back on the ground he beamed. It was one of his best experiences ever, he said.

In Vietnam Ben was the radio operator on a Green Beret long range reconnaissance patrol team that routinely spent six weeks or more at a time in the Vietnamese and Cambodian jungle. He once told me about coming face to face with a Viet Cong. "He pulled back the grass and I pulled back the grass and we were looking across a little opening at each other," Ben said. "I let the grass go and he let the grass go and we both just melted back into the jungle." Ben didn't talk much about the war and when he did it was with his usual good humor and humility. His war stories were about soldiers he knew and places he saw and good times.

After the Army he married Sue, a beautiful Columbus County girl, and finished his education at the University of Georgia. He became a successful business executive, at one time managing three building supply plants in the Carolinas. Ben's father and his friends from Horry County liked to fish the big water, the Santee-Cooper lakes, in particular, but we liked the small water, places where you could paddle through the underbrush to find a little body of water hidden in the swamp among the cypress knees and a secluded campsite. We liked to float water that flowed ever so slowly, like the way we talked. He, Gene and I hoped one day to live in such a place again. We would each buy a house on the river and go back into the swamps anytime we wanted. In later years, we were always comfortable returning to our little corner of paradise in Nichols.

That flight up the Lumber was the genesis for our planned float trip on the two rivers we loved. When his new cancer was diagnosed shortly afterwards I started planning harder, convinced that the more positive we all were about the trip, the more we could help him with his recovery. After his radiation treatments began he could barely talk and Sue was our go-between. When I called from overseas she relayed the news that he was dedicated to getting stronger for the trip.

In late November 2010 after he had completed two months of chemotherapy and radiation, I called from Italy to get an update. "He's sitting right here with me and he can talk," Sue said. Ben came on the line. "I've been reading what you've written about the river," he began. "On our trip we'll take it easy. We're not young anymore. But it will be good. I'll take my cooker. We'll stop on a sandbar, have a good rest."

Gene and I always wanted to sleep in our own beds. But Ben insisted on pitching a tent, gathering wood, building a fire, cooking fish and celebrating life by talking about experiences. He was right, as usual. A little discomfort just served to make the experiences more memorable. We set the trip down the Lumber from Fair Bluff for low water in the early summer of 2011 and I planned to come home in February to get my gear set up and make a plan with two more cousins who would join us. But when I got home Ben was at the end and all I could do was make the promise to complete the trip for him.

On the river now with Chick, my mind wandered to Ben's eulogy. I told our family and friends at his church service in Youngsville, N.C., that "Ben will always be there for me in the warmth of a glorious summer night on the river, when the world was 16, when we were, for the briefest of moments, immortal. He lives on in the remembrance of a boyish smile and a mischievous laugh that lasted a lifetime, in the steel of his courage; in his Green Beret, in the constancy of never forgetting a friend or failing to keep a promise, in the faces of his children and grandchildren, in the indelible memories of a brave and gentle man who did his duty to his family, to his country and to his God. We will love you forever Ben, and there will never be a day in which we do not smile at the thought of how your life touched ours and made us better for having known you."

Chick brought me back to the present with details on the distinctive crescent shaped white sandbars of the Lumber and the Little Pee Dee. He explained that they form in high water when the power of the river deposits tons of sand onto the inside bend. Many of the sandbars are brilliant white, quartz sand, whiter than even those of the Carolina Sandhills and rivaling the white beauty of the state's best Atlantic beaches. Opposite the sandbars, the swift, dark water on the outside turn cuts a deep path, eroding the shoreline, often toppling mature trees which fall across the channel. The trees and their massive roots block the normal paddling route, often forcing sharply angled turns from one side of the river to the other.

On the sandbar where we had stopped, Chick pointed out what I knew as a Cowkiller Ant as it scurried under a log at our feet. It's not a big red ant, he said, but a wasp without wings, *Dasymutilla occidentalis*, sometimes called the Velvet Ant. The female, which can be three-quarters of an inch long, lays her eggs in the ground nests of bees and her young, in nature's brutally efficient scheme of survival, eat the bee's offspring for nourishment.

Until this trip I would have told you there had been only three bridges on this section of the Lumber, the 904 crossing at Fair Bluff, the railroad trestle above Nichols and the S.C. Highway 9-76 Bridge near the Nichols town limit sign. But less than a mile below Cora's Landing we paddled up to the weathered pilings of what had been another bridge over the river. Closer inspection revealed two rows of pilings about six feet apart, apparently all that remains of a logging tram bridge built more than a century before to haul out timber.

The primary method in the 18th and 19th centuries of getting the timber to lumber mills was via the river. Trees up to 100 feet in length were strapped together and guided down the Lumber into the Little Pee Dee and Great Pee Dee all the way to Georgetown for milling. The bridge pilings we found are unmarked and pose a danger to all boats, particularly in high water when most of the posts are submerged. I had never crossed this section of the river at low water and thus had floated or motored across the pilings several times without knowing they were there.

There is no longer any reason to keep the river clear for logging traffic and fallen trees often stretch halfway across the channel. Trees that floated down the river and then lodged in midstream pose another hazard to unwary boaters. The biggest logs and uprooted trees in the main channel are often marked with a warning, usually a broken boat paddle or length of wood with a red flag or pennant tacked to the end.

Marion County begins on the west bank just below the remains of the wood bridge and a little over a mile further we paddled under high voltage power lines that mark the beginning of the final run into Nichols. We came alongside Huggins Lake, which is hidden off to the right in the swamp, and then rounded the last bend before the Nichols railroad trestle at 14 miles downriver.

The trestle walk was a rite of passage for boys and girls growing up during my youth in Nichols. The initiate had to cross the trestle alone, walking from crosstie to crosstie with the dark water sliding past menacingly 20 feet below between the openings. All I could think of on my first crossing as a nine-year-old was that my legs would go through and I'd be stuck there until the train cut me in half. The fear almost paralyzed me. And at the height of the tension, midway any first-time trestle walk, someone always screamed, "Train, the freight train, it's coming! Run!" There was no train, but reminiscent of the scene in the movie *Stand by Me*, there was the same panic to get off the trestle.

Until the end of scheduled passenger service along the line nearly forty years ago, trains ran daily with regular service from Wilmington, Charlotte and other large cities into Nichols, Mullins and Marion and on to Columbia. Now there is only an occasional freight train on this section of track. And the trestle on the other side of town, connecting Nichols with Mullins over the Little Pee Dee, has been periodically closed to traffic in recent years because of structural concerns.

Both Marion and Mullins preserved the classic red brick train stations that marked the stops along the route of what was the Atlantic Coast Line Railroad when I was young. Both stations now house museums. But the town fathers of Nichols failed to have as much foresight and allowed the station to be torn down.

Our trusty chauffeur C.P. had been in touch by cell phone and promised to be at the Nichols Bridge arrival point on time. We talked to him while passing Round Hole Lake on the east side and then Fishtrap Lake a bend further on the same side.

Two hundred feet above Nichols Bridge at Ward's Slough, almost 16 miles downriver, we climbed out onto the sandy bank. Ten minutes later we heard the rumble of C.P.'s diesel coming down the river road. At five, after a half day on the river, we shoved everything into the back of the pickup and headed out. Our uncle wanted a full report and we regaled him with tales of the river. As noted earlier, it is a family tradition not to let the truth get in the way of a good story and we hewed to tradition in our accounts of the day. There was enough to report that we had hope of earning an invitation to a supper cooked by Aunt Betty. A meal at her table usually means a plate of speckled butterbeans, fried okra, homemade sausage or a grilled pork chop, delicate hand-rolled biscuits and a pitcher of dark, strong, iced tea. Afterwards for the adventurous comes a glass of homemade red wine and a shot of moonshine from C.P.'s secret stash.

I am convinced hard work plus the wine, the 'shine' and a determination to squeeze the juice from each day have kept my uncle young as he nears his ninth decade. My aunt also. They promise the formula will work for us and we are almost true believers. I do hope they are right. And that we reach such an advanced age with their zest for the next adventure.

But whatever the future holds, it cannot diminish the pleasure of this day, one dedicated to fulfilling a promise to my cousin Ben.

Ben Brown (l) and the four daughters and grandchildren of Carroll Eugene 'Gene' Connelly, Jr., join on the Lumber River in 2009 to send Gene's ashes downriver.

Gene Connelly asked that his ashes be spread on the Lumber River. Photo courtesy of family

Nichols Bridge to Fork Retch

We returned in a few weeks for our second day on the Lumber and shoved off from the same spot above Nichols Bridge where in 2009 I had helped spread my Cousin Gene's Connelly's ashes on the river. He had asked that his four daughters, grandchildren and friends say goodbye at the place where he had spent many of the best times of his youth. That day I had done my part by throwing a handful of ashes high into the air. I watched them float to the surface of the dark water and wished my cousin a good journey down to Georgetown and on to eternity.

Chick's son Lin joined us for the trip and moved far ahead with powerful strokes, then slowed for us to catch up before once again pushing on downstream. Chick and I kept our kayaks headed downriver and let the current do the work, playing tortoise to Lin's hare until, we speculated, the unseasonably warm weather would reel him in as the sun climbed overhead.

The 1948 U.S. Geological Survey map of this section shows only 17 major bends in the four-mile stretch of the Lumber between Nichols and the junction with the Little Pee Dee. That made it the simplest section of water we would encounter in our exploration of the two rivers. At the same time it would also be one of the most scenic stretches of either river.

I learned to scuba dive off Bathhouse Cove, the broad bend a quarter mile below the Highway 76 Bridge. Once, in a not so rare moment of youthful stupidity, I intentionally frightened a woman fishing on the bank there by emerging from the water near her fishing line in swim fins, mask and air tank. It seemed like a good idea until I did it.

Beyond the next sandbar on the left a flood diversion canal which begins near Fair Bluff enters the river on the Horry side. The next bend is Rice Field Cove. In my youth it was a landing known as a barren, sinister place with a powerful current responsible for several drownings. In the intervening years a collection of homes and a boat motor repair garage went up near the paved ramp put in by the county. Across the river the sandbar at Rice Field had been a good, private place for boys like us to camp. Ben once caught a five-pound Alligator garfish, *Atractosteus spatula,* off the upper end of the sandbar after a long battle using a little Zebco reel, a Mepps spinner and fragile, four-pound- test line. And Gene built a campfire that lasted all that summer night.

For the next mile we glided past thick, lowland forest that grew right up to the Marion County bank. The Horry side was clear cut a few years ago, a reminder of the latest development in man's alteration of the landscape in a place where the natural beauty begs for preservation. Those who love the river sometimes tell visitors that what they are seeing is the same natural backdrop witnessed by the Indians in the time before European explorers came. That is not the case as much of the timber has been culled three to four times, roads cut into previously undeveloped areas and clearings cut away for cabins and homes. It remains beautiful, but certainly not pristine. The Indians and early explorers saw something else, grander, more beautiful and wild.

With Lin still paddling out front, we encountered another classic oxbow two miles downriver from Nichols Bridge. Here the Lumber meanders nearly 90 degrees to the west and then turns back sharply to form a classic oxbow. The Geological Survey Map done in 1948 three years after my birth shows the channel moving right as it approaches a finger lake on the Horry side. A little more than a half century later the river now flows directly into what had been the finger lake at the base of the oxbow. I ran this section of river at extreme high water the previous year and the narrow cut-through where the river now carves an ever widening main channel offered no more than ten feet of opening as the swift current surged between a gauntlet of fallen trees and overhanging brush. That contrasted sharply with this morning's gentle movement of the current between the fallen trees.

We turned west into the oxbow and taunts were exchanged about who would be the first to monkey walk, the first forced to use his hands to push along the sandy bottom clearly visible in the tea-colored flow. Lin scooted across the entrance while Chick shoved his paddle deep in the sand and simultaneously lifted himself in the air, launching his green kayak over the sand hump. I heard scraping but cleared the bar. We passed through the oxbow and down to the second bend afterwards, 3.1 miles downriver. The log cabin on that bend was not there in my youth. It was built in more recent years by the family that once owned the 1,000 acre parcel of land stretching from Highway 76 Bridge for nearly four miles. A year earlier I saw a real estate ad offering the whole parcel for about $1,200 an acre.

At the end of the first right-hand bend after passing the cabin we paddled level with the entrance to Widow's Lake, a fishing spot connected by a hidden water entrance that neither Chick nor Lin was aware of. I nosed my kayak into an opening between cypress knees and overhanging brush on the west bank and probed the water depth with my paddle. It was still more than six inches, enough for us to easily float in. We glided silently along a three-foot corridor flanked by algae-covered cypress knees and a wall of tree trunks that seemingly barred the entrance until you were into the hidden channel.

We emerged into a body of water no more than 70 feet across, perhaps 700 feet long and encircled by cypresses. Sunlight penetrated the thick tree canopy in a striated pattern, painting successive bands of light and shadow on the water. Fish rolled at half a dozen spots along the lake and something fell into the water. Too early in the year to be a snake, Chick said.

Widow's Lake was once a favorite camping trek for local boys in a long-ago time when posted signs in the area were rare on private land and usually ignored because everyone knew the Nichols family, who owned most of the acreage around the town. The walk to the lake and the river covered several miles and first passed alongside the 3,000-foot grass runway at Nichols airport, less than a mile from the river.

The airstrip was built in the early 1950s by a group of local pilots spearheaded by Randolph Battle and Euel Shelley. The airport quickly became a center for general aviation in the Pee Dee Region east of Florence. It was abandoned in the 1970's after the construction of Marion County regional airport between Mullins and Marion.

I told Chick and Lin about the time spent at the airport with my dad, a pilot for the Civil Air Patrol, and Chick recalled Huggins Memorial Field in Timmonsville, where veteran crop duster M.B. 'Dusty' Huggins ran the show. Huggins

Memorial, unlike Nichols, is still an active airfield. Both Dusty Huggins and Randolph Battle are in the South Carolina Aviation Hall of Fame.

Lin got tired of our reminiscing and paddled for the exit channel. As we left single file I pointed out the rusted sheets of tin nailed to a rotting wood frame on the high ground above us. This, I told Chick and Lin, was once the river dwelling of a man named Sco Butler, who my dad always called a hermit. But C.P. said he was just a fisherman who enjoyed the river and lived in the shack while catching fish he later sold.

After Widow's Lake the channel opened up in a wide curve with a fine sandbar on the west bank. In a little more than a mile of paddling through a half dozen bends we were at Anderson Lake, a finger of the river reaching back nearly 800 feet into the woods on the Marion side. This had once been a good fishing lake with Bream and Morgans. Now it was filled with Mudfish.

It was on Anderson Lake, according to often-retold Walker family legend, that Sheldon, one of my father's brothers, walked on water many years before. When a snake dropped from a low-hanging limb into the boat at his feet, Sheldon crossed boat to stump to limb to cypress knee to the bank without getting a drop of water on himself. That left my dad alone with the snake. According to my dad's telling of the tale, he lifted the Red-bellied Water Snake out of the boat and paddled to shore to pick up Sheldon. If it had been a poisonous moccasin, I'm sure he would have tried to duplicate Sheldon's jump out of the boat.

Lin paddled ahead as usual as we exited Anderson Lake and glided directly into a submerged sand bank on the river side of the lake entrance. He was stuck and would have to either monkey walk or get out and pull. He chose to stay in his craft and started pushing with his palms in the water, ignoring our razzing.

An eighth of a mile below Anderson Lake, the fastest flowing part of the Lumber cuts through a spit of land and prematurely joins the Little Pee Dee. I showed Chick and Lin the bubbles created by the swift action of the water curling into the hidden cutoff and its entrance between two mature cypresses. The flow took hold of our kayaks one after the other and drew us into a swirling eddy that seemed to drop like rapids between the cypress knees and the trees. One second the trees and bushes whizzed by and the next our kayaks popped out on the placid Little Pee Dee.

It was mid-afternoon as we lined up alongside each other facing the open water. The current began to pull us downstream into the much stronger flow of a river three times the width of the Little Pee before its junction with the Lumber. We floated across the sandbar where the two rivers joined and into Fork Retch. We were 5.16 miles from Nichols and 21.5 miles down from Fair Bluff.

That night at our house on The Retch I toasted the Green Berets, knocking back a shot of C.P.'s most potent 120 proof clear 'moon', followed immediately by iced tea. My eyes watered not only from the burn of the alcohol but also from the flood of good memories.

Lin Gaddy of Columbia paddles along the narrow entrance to Widow's Lake below Nichols on the Lumber River.

The tannin-stained Little Pee Dee joins the muddy Great Pee Dee at the tip of Britton's Neck near where Marion, Georgetown and Horry counties meet.

17

Flying The River

In late November 2013, with the kayaks put away until spring, I decided on one more trip down the Little Pee Dee. I would fly from Red Bluff Lake to the Tanyard, following the river as closely as I could from the air. I picked a perfect day, a Monday with blue skies and 20 miles plus visibility. The outside thermometer gauge on my old single engine Cessna read 33 degrees Fahrenheit at 1,500 feet as I made the 27-mile flight from my home airfield, Marion Regional, to Red Bluff Lake on the outskirts of Clio. I was above the lake in fifteen minutes and circled to start my run down the river.

Chick and I had begun there in February, a thousand feet below on the spillway. The Little Pee Dee spread out in front of my aircraft reaching to the horizon as a gray, green and orange belt of fall and winter foliage that uncoiled to the east. I flew with the aircraft control wheel in my left hand and a digital camera in my right.

I knew the trip would be relatively brief at 100 mph, but I had not imagined how quickly the first part would pass. We labored for five different days on the river to get down from Red Bluff to Dillon. Now, enroute only eight minutes from the headwaters, I could see Interstate 95 on the outskirts of the city. Shortly after crossing the interstate I deviated around the two television towers that mark the eastern entrance to Dillon about 1.5 miles from Highway 57 and the Dillon County Landing on the river. In another nine minutes I passed over Mosquito Beach, our favorite stopping point on the river alongside the Mincey farm. Ahead, Fork Retch rolled out as a long dark strip of water among the cypresses. Another TV tower near the Retch pushed me to the East.

In five minutes the construction on the Sandy Bluff Bridge below was clear in great detail as was the spot where Quincey Strickland had hooked his last fish. Four minutes later I was above the Highway 501 Bridge at Galivants Ferry where my kayak fell off C.P.'s pickup at the end of one long day on the river. In the distance I could clearly make out the ever-widening river belt as it headed into Lower Marion County. The great, relatively unspoiled Woodbury Tract, nearly 26,000 acres in all, came up on my right as I passed over Potato Bed Ferry and the new U.S. Highway 378 Bridge.

The dramatic spread of the river into three channels below Punch Bowl Landing had been extraordinary on the water and was now even more beautiful from the air. The swamp appeared more than two miles across, with the main river clearly outlined on the left, a separate middle channel and the Russ Creek cut-through that passes the Tree House on the right. I passed over several fishing boats on the flight. They were tiny shapes in the water and more than once I saw reflections as fishermen in sunglasses looked skyward. From our long days on the river, I was almost smug in my knowledge of where they were, what boat landing they were nearest, what the river was like exactly where they were fishing. Finally the channels merged and swept the flow of the Little Pee Dee into the reddish brown Great Pee Dee. I circled the junction and saw, as always, that the black water and red did not mingle immediately, rather continued separate paths downstream for probably half a mile before the Great Pee Dee ended all traces of its tributary.

I completed my circle of the junction at 2:27 p.m. The paddling trip that consumed over 160 hours had been completed unhurriedly by air in 43 minutes.

The unfolding view of the river, the expanse of green belt that winds to the horizon, the live view from above cannot be duplicated by satellite photo, video or any other medium. The same holds true for seeing the extraordinary beauty of Eastern South Carolina. To watch as the rivers, the farms, fields, cities and towns slide under the wing of a light aircraft flying low and slow is a pleasure every person should experience at least once in a lifetime. The flight complemented but could never replace the adventure of paddling the river.

Twenty minutes later I was on approach for Marion County Airport. It is normally a fairly sleepy place with a limited number of takeoffs and landings. But on the radio this day a single engine Mooney aircraft announced it was inbound from the north. The Air Reach medevac helicopter that works from the field was approaching from the west. And I was coming from the south. I throttled back and waited for the other two craft to land. This flight marked the end of my Little Pee Dee journey and I had no objection to it lasting a few minutes longer.

The river trip had consumed most of my free time for more than a year and I had learned a great deal in that time. Although I would never possess my Cousin Chick's knowledge about plant and animal life, I sensed I was now closing in on him with respect to my appreciation of nature. That happened because I had been gifted, like all those around me in the Pee Dee, with a stunning, Southern jewel of a river at my doorstep and with the opportunity to trace first hand a remarkable chapter of history written by a genuine American hero named Francis Marion and his hardy band of volunteers.

Chick and I had not only paddled the river of our youth, we had revisited our country's history and that of our family. And we had taken time to cherish those departed and to learn from those who remained. The two of us were now not only close relatives, but closer friends. As men we were more than we had been when the journey began. These things, I am certain, mark the real achievement of our magical days on the Little Pee Dee.

The branches of the lower Little Pee Dee (left) join into one wide channel a short distance upriver from the junction with the Great Pee Dee.

18
Map annex
Little Pee Dee North

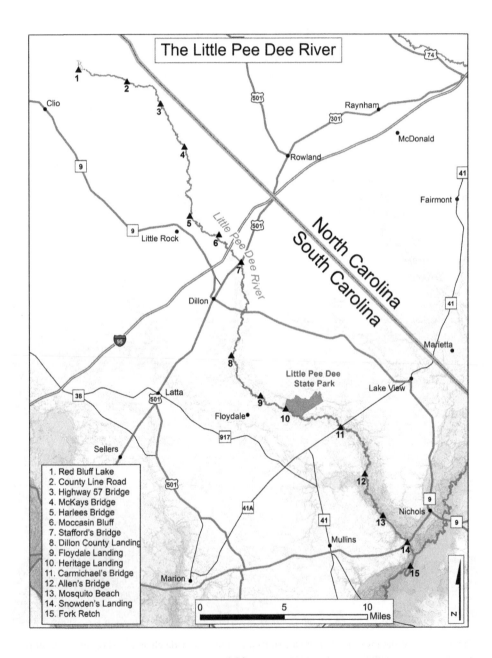

Little Pee Dee South

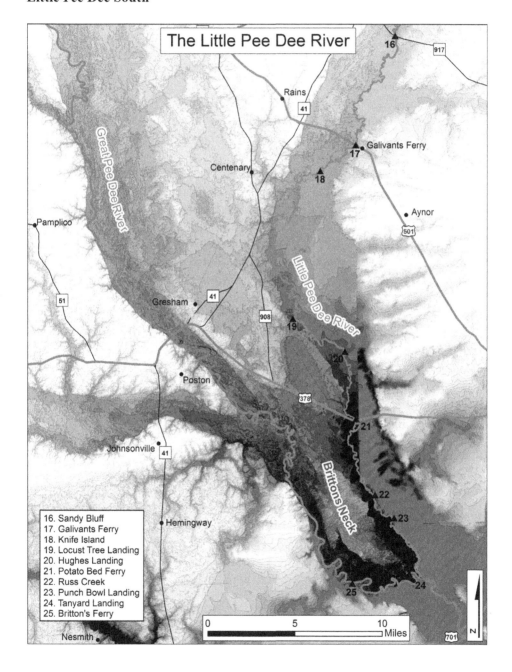

Bibliography

Able, Gene and Jack Horan. *Paddling South Carolina A Guide to Palmetto State River Trails*. Orangeburg, S.C.,: Sandlapper Publishing Co. Inc. 1986.

Alsop, Fred J. III. *Birds of North America Eastern Region*. New York: DK Publishing, Inc., 2001.

Bass, Jack and Scott Poole. *The Palmetto State The Making of Modern South Carolina*. Columbia, S.C.,: University of South Carolina Press. 2009.

Bass, Robert D. *Swamp Fox, The life and campaigns of GENERAL FRANCIS MARION*. Orangeburg, S.C.: Sandlapper Publishing Co, Inc., 1959.

Boating Guide to the Little Pee Dee, Scenic River Water Trail in Dillon County, South Carolina Department of Natural Resources.

Burroughs, Franklin. *The River Home A Return to the Carolina Low Country*. Athens, Ga.,: University of Georgia Press, 1992.

Cornelius, Kay. *Francis Marion The Swamp Fox* (Revolutionary War Leaders Series). Philadelphia, Pa.,: Chelsea House Publishers, 2003.

Dickey, James, *Deliverance*. New York: Dell Publishing Co. 1970.

Eastman, John. *The Book of Swamp and Bog Trees, Shrubs and Wildflowers of Eastern Freshwater Wetlands*. Mechanicsburg, Pa.,: Stackpole Books, 1995.

Edgar, Walter. *South Carolina A History*. Columbia, S.C.,: University of South Carolina Press, 1998.

_____, editor. *The South Carolina Encyclopedia*. Columbia, S.C.,: University of South Carolina Press, 2006.

Gaddy, L.L. with John E Cely. *The Natural History of Congaree Swamp*. Columbia, S.C.,: terra incognita books, 2012.

_____. *Spiders of the Carolinas American Naturalist Series*. Duluth, MN.,: Kollath and Stensaas Publishing, 2009

Garren, Laura Ann. *The Chattooga River A Natural & Cultural History*. Charleston, S.C.: Natural History Press, 2013.

Geffen, Alice M. *A Birdwatcher's Guide to the Eastern United States*. Woodbury, N.Y.,: Barron's Publishing. 1978.

Lane, John. *My Paddle To The Sea. Eleven Days on the River of the Carolinas.* Athens, Ga,: University of Georgia Press, 2011.

Lewis, Catherine H. *Horry County, South Carolina 1730-1993.* University of South Carolina Press, 1998.

Robertson, Ben. *Red Hills and Cotton An Upcountry Memory.* Columbia, S.C.: University of South Carolina Press, 1963.

Rutledge, Archibald. *Home By The River.* Columbia, S.C.,: New edition, Sandlapper Press, Inc., 1970.

Wallace, David Duncan. *South Carolina A Short History.* Columbia, S.C.,: University of South Carolina Press, 1961.

Zeigler, Norm. *Rivers of Shadow Rivers of Sun A Fly-Fisher's European Journal.* Camden, Maine. Countrysport Press, 2004.

National Audubon Society. *Field Guide To Trees Eastern Region, North America.* New York: Chanticleer Press, 1980.

Notes

1. The Gum Swamp and Beaver Creek drainages flow nearly 10 miles down from the Laurinburg, N.C. area across the state line into Marlboro County, S.C., before entering Red Bluff Lake. The stream emerging from the lake is considered the actual beginning of the Little Pee Dee. An underground spillway on the east side and an above ground spillway on the north side of the lake mouth regulate the lake level.
2. The casual pollution of the river is probably the single greatest threat to its continued use for tourism. As the eddies of trash grow the beauty of paddling the river diminishes.
3. The Pee Dee Land Trust (http://www.peedeelandtrust.org/) is a nonprofit public interest organization dedicated to conserving and promoting an appreciation of the significant natural, agricultural and historical resources of the Pee Dee Region. It focuses on the nine South Carolina counties—Chesterfield, Darlington, Dillon, Florence, Georgetown, Horry, Marion, Marlboro and Williamsburg—that border the Great Pee Dee River from the North Carolina line to the Atlantic Ocean.
4. http://www.dillonheraldonline.com/2010/12/13/michelle-lee-brown/
5. *Boating Guide to the Little Pee Dee, Scenic River Water Trail in Dillon County*, South Carolina Department of Natural Resources, p.59.
6. A good place to find historic marker citations for South Carolina is the Latitude 34 North website, http://lat34north.com/HistoricMarkersSC/CountyMap.cfm Click on any of the state's 46 counties and get a listing of all the historic markers there and the citations.
7. http://www.peedeeindiantribeofsc.com/id3.html
8. See also the Pee Dee Indian Nation of Beaver Creek, another state recognized tribe primarily in Orangeburg County along the Edisto River. Its headquarters is at Salley, S.C.
9. Pee Dee Indian Tribe website.
10. See Town Creek Indian Mound, http://www.nchistoricsites.org/town/town.htm The web site notes, "In the southern North Carolina Piedmont, the clearest expression of South Appalachian Mississippian tradition is the Pee Dee culture. And the most obvious archaeological site relating to the Pee Dee culture

is the Town Creek site, located on the Little River in Montgomery County."
11. American Bison were reported in the South Carolina Piedmont as late as the early 1700s.
12. http://www.dnr.sc.gov/wildlife/wetlands/carolinabays.html   DNR notes that "The Carolina Bay is sometimes called 'pocosin' which is the Indian word for "swamp on a hill." Bay swamps were so-called due to an abundance of bay trees. Carolina Bays are oriented in a northwest-southeast, shoreline-perpendicular direction and parallel to one another. DNR's also has made available online a study by Stephen H. Bennett and John B. Nelson titled *Distribution and Status of Carolina Bays in South Carolina* (http://www.dnr.sc.gov/wildlife/docs/CarolinaBaysStudy.pdf).
13. Gardening Know How, Growing and Caring for Cardinal Flowers, Jackie Carroll,   http://www.gardeningknowhow.com/ornamental/flowers/cardinal-flower/growing-cardinal-flowers.htm
14. The back road leaving Nichols and continuing past the local golf course to Mullins is often called Old Mullins Highway. It is also known by many as Old Nichols Highway. It is officially State Road S-34-60.
15. A winter 1973 article from The Sandlapper Magazine ("Ancient Ferrymen On Little Pee Dee") written by then South Carolina Commissioner of Agriculture William L. Harrelson of Mullins, provides additional information on Little Pee Dee Landings and particularly on events at Huggins Landing.
16. Copyright: Bro 'N Sis Music Inc.
17. Little Pee Dee Lodge has been reopened and then closed as a restaurant several times in recent years. In spring 2014, at the time this book was completed, it was closed.
18. Norm Zeigler, *Rivers of Shadow, Rivers of Sun, A Fly-Fisher's European Journal* (Camden, Maine: Countrysport Press, 2004)
19. Old Stage Road provides a short cut from highway 76 outside Nichols to Highway 917 connecting Mullins with Horry County via the Sandy Bluff Highway Bridge.
20. http://www.sctrails.net/trails/ALLTRAILS/WaterTrails/LittlePeeDeeHP.html
21. At Thanksgiving 2013, a family friend, Ken Foster, presented C.P. and my Cousin Ken with an inscribed plank which commemorated the date of the cabin construction and the work by L.G. Page in dismantling, moving and reassembling the cabin.
22. Joint U.S. Geological Survey/S.C. Department of Natural Resources measurement.
23. Liberty County, once a part of the large Georgetown District, existed for thirteen years, from 1785-1798, until it became Marion District/County in honor of Francis Marion. Kingston County, also once a part of the Georgetown district, took the name Horry District/County in 1801, honoring one of Gen. Marion's key Revolutionary War subordinates, Sir Peter Horry.

24. The Tory, or Crown, supporters were numerous in an area defined by Catfish Creek outside the town of Marion and along the present-day boundaries of Gilchrist Road above the Little Pee Dee near the current C.P. Mincey and Norman Huggins farms, stretching six miles to the Lake View area and then east across to the present-day town of Nichols along Drowning Creek.
25. Robert D. Bass, *Swamp Fox, The life and campaigns of GENERAL FRANCIS MARION* (Sandlapper Publishing Co, Inc., 1959), 51.
26. Robert A. Pierce in the *South Carolina Encyclopedia* (p. 355) edited by Walter Edgar reports, "The meetings were started in a place called "the Thicket" by Press Daniels, area Democratic club president and executive committeeman. They matured into a tradition under the guidance of the Holliday family. The "stump," which referred to a time when politicians promoted their candidacy by allegedly giving speeches while standing on tree stumps, was moved to a site beside the Holliday family store and continued by four generations of Hollidays...."
27. The Galivants Ferry Historic District is listed in the National Register of Historic Places. For more information see the brochure *Galivants Ferry* or view it online at: http://www.horrycounty.org/boards/bar/GalivantsFerry.asp
28. L.L. Gaddy, *Ferns of the West Indies*, eBook (PDF) lulu.com; iBook, http://www.itunes.com/, 129 pages.
29. The geographic area and community of Brittons Neck is commonly spelled without the possessive. This includes usage in the South Carolina Atlas & Gazetteer. But Britton's Ferry is commonly spelled with the possessive. And the state historic marker for the community uses Britton's Neck.
30. A 125-foot cypress in Florida was thought to be the world's oldest cypress, at more than 3,500 years. The tree, in the Big Tree Park in Longwood, Fla., was destroyed in a fire on Jan. 16, 2012. The tree was reputed to be the oldest Pond Bald Cypress in the U.S. and the fifth oldest tree on the Earth. See Philip Caulfield, New York Daily News, Feb. 29, 2012, *"Florida police arrest woman in arson fire that destroyed 3,500-year-old tree, known as 'The Senator.'* http://www.nydailynews.com/news/national/florida-police-arrest-woman-arson-fire-destroyed-3-500-year-old-tree-senator-article-1.1030373
31. Eliza Lucas Pinckney, Distinguished Women of Past and Present, http://www.distinguishedwomen.com/biographies/pinckney.html
32. Robert D. Bass, Swamp Fox, The life and campaigns of GENERAL FRANCIS MARION (Sandlapper Publishing Co, Inc., 1959).
33. Waldo H. Tres Hyman is a timber consultant with offices in Marion, S.C. Hyman has been active in researching Revolutionary War sites for many years and widely recognized as one of the most knowledgeable individuals about the Pee Dee countryside where Francis Marion and his men fought the British and Tory supporters.
34. *Water Tupelo* by R.L. Johnson, Northeastern Area State & Private Forestry, http://na.fs.fed.us/pubs/silvics_manual/volume_2/nyssa/aquatica.htm

35. Bob Barrett of Florence completed his duties as Trail Commission chairman in 2012. He continues to be active in historical projects connected to Francis Marion and the Great and Little Pee Dee Rivers.
36. http://www.nature.org/ourinitiatives/regions/northamerica/unitedstates/south-carolina/placesweprotect/woodbury-tract.xml
37. http:////wildlifeaction.com/

Order additional copies of
Down The Little Pee Dee
online at http://www.wswbooks.com

About the Paddlers

William S. Walker is a South Carolina-born author with a lifelong interest in the state's Pee Dee region and Revolutionary War leader Francis Marion, the Swamp Fox. Walker, from Nichols in Marion County, worked as a reporter and editor in the United States and Europe for more than four decades and has written and edited for newspapers on assignments in over 50 countries. He began a 28-year career with the newspaper *Stars and Stripes* at Darmstadt, Germany, as a reporter in 1973 and was the newspaper's worldwide Executive Editor when he retired in 2002. Before joining Stars and Stripes Walker worked at daily newspapers in South Carolina and as a news editor for the Associated Press. He is a graduate of Clemson University, the University of South Carolina and Ruprecht-Karls-Universität in Heidelberg, Germany, where he earned a Ph.D. in East European History. His 2010 book, *German and Bosnian Voices In A Time Of Crisis*, told the story of Bosnian refugees in Germany from 1992-2002. Walker is currently researching for a book on South Carolina politics.

L.L. "Chick" Gaddy, a native of Timmonsville, South Carolina, is a naturalist and author based in Columbia, S.C. He is a graduate of the University of South Carolina and holds a Ph. D. in biogeography from the University of Georgia. Gaddy is president of the environmental consulting firm terra incognita. He has done environmental-related studies on endangered species, wetlands and conservation from Maine to Idaho during a nearly 40-year career. His interest in the Pee Dee region begun more than a half century ago during fishing trips with his father on the Little Pee Dee River. Gaddy's other books include: *The Natural History of the Congaree Swamp* (2013) *Ferns of the West Indies* (2013) *Spiders of the Carolinas* (2009), *Biodiversity: Przewalski's horse, Edna's trillium, the giant squid, and over 1.5 million other species* (2005) and a *Naturalist's Guide to the Blue Ridge Front* (2000).

CPSIA information can be obtained at www.ICGtesting.com
Printed in the USA
LVOW02s1733230115

423970LV00008B/11/P